BOOK H
READING FOR CONCEPTS

"Today is not yesterday."   Carlyle

WILLIAM LIDDLE

General Editor
Director, Instructional Services
Colorado Springs Public Schools
Director of the Reading Clinic, the Colorado College
Colorado Springs, Colorado

BOOK H READING

FOR CONCEPTS

Second Edition

WEBSTER DIVISION
McGRAW-HILL BOOK COMPANY

New York   St. Louis   San Francisco
Auckland   Bogotá   Düsseldorf   Johannesburg   London   Madrid
Mexico   Montreal   New Delhi   Panama   Paris   São Paulo
Singapore   Sydney   Tokyo   Toronto

Contributing Authors for the Reading for Concepts Series:

Linda Barton, feature writer for *St. Louis Today.*

Roberta H. Berry, elementary school teacher, writer.

Barbara Broeking, journalist and educational publications editor.

Eth Clifford, author of many volumes of fiction and poetry for youth.

Ellen Dolan, juvenile book author.

Barbara R. Frey, Professor of Education, State University College, Buffalo, N.Y.

Ruth Harley, author and editor of young people's periodicals.

Phyllis W. Kirk, children's book editor.

Richard Kirk, author of science, social studies, and reading books for youth.

Thomas D. Mantel, attorney and juvenile author.

Marilyn F. Peachin, journalist and editor.

James N. Rogers, author-editor of science and social studies resource books.

James J. Pflaum, author and editor of current events periodicals.

Gloria S. Rosenzweig, writer of primary teaching materials.

Jean Shirley, author of juvenile books.

Rosemary Winebrenner, editor of children's books.

Jean White, journalist and writer of young people's reference materials.

Educational Consultant:

Dr. Ruth Gallant, The Center for Teaching and Learning, University of North Dakota, Grand Forks, N.D.

Statisticians for Original Prepublication Field Trials:

Dr. Michael Grady and Dr. Roslyn Grady, Colorado Springs, Colo.

Robert Hampson, Pupil Accounting and Testing Services, Colorado Springs, Colo.

Resource Committee:

Ruth Liddle, Eleanor Wier, Ruth Mitchell, Jean Keeley, and Joseph Tockman.

Project Editor: Carol Washburne
Designer: Jim Darby
Editing Supervisor: Sal Allocco
Production Supervisor: Karen Romano

Illustrators: James Cummings; Portia Takajian, GAI
Cover Photo: Erich Hartmann/Magnum

ISBN 0-07-037668-9

TABLE OF CONTENTS

Purpose

This book is the last of eight in the series "Reading for Concepts." It was designed to provide an opportunity for young readers to grow in reading experience while exploring a wide variety of ideas contained in several of the academic disciplines.

Four basic underlying concepts are reflected in this book. They are: *Change may produce unexpected results. Some changes are planned; others are accidental. Modern ways of life require planned change,* and *Where might change take us?* The overriding concept in this book relates to elements of creativity and possibilities for new movements in the future.

To illustrate these concepts, stories have been written around intriguing pieces of information which reflect these ideas. The content has been drawn from the ten disciplines of history, space, biology, anthropology, economics, geography, earth science, mathematics, engineering, and art.

Two stories are presented in each discipline. A narrative follows after stories 20, 40, and 60. The narratives, two from folk literature and one science fiction, will provide a change of pace and are "just for fun" types of stories.

Teaching Procedure

The child should be given a diagnostic test (see the teacher's manual) at the beginning of the program to help the teacher in determining at which reading level he is operating, and the best book to begin in the series.

1. Discuss the title and picture clue in the story and establish purposes for reading it.

2. Present difficult words in advance. (There is an index at the back of this book which will direct the teacher in selecting the words expected to cause difficulties at each reading level.)

3. Have students read the story silently. A timed approach may be useful for more skillful readers. The stories are all approximately 270–300 words long. Narratives lengths are listed. Begin with a reading time suitable to the average needs of the group. Moderate speed in reading is an indication of reading proficiency, but it is not the basic province of this series. As comprehension increases, the emphasis may switch to reducing reading time. At this time, use a stopwatch and figure each reader's rate for a story and encourage him to read more quickly each subsequent time. By using the charts he can see his own progress.

4. Following each regular story is a test which is especially designed to improve specific skills in reading. There are charts at the end of this book on which to record scores for each skill tested. By carefully using these charts, teacher and pupil can make a diagnosis of specific skill weaknesses and also keep track of progress in each aspect of reading skill.

The sample exercise that begins the pupil's text should be reviewed carefully with all pupils. Each test item in the sample should be examined. Pupils should understand in advance exactly how they are to arrive at correct answers, whether they are expected to retain information, to verify from the text, to find the exact word needed, or to conjecture on the basis of information given. Success is necessary. The sample exercise will be found at the end of this discussion.

The skills tested in Book H are typical of those suggested in Bloom's *Taxonomy of Educational Objectives.* Bloom's Taxonomy is a way of ordering thinking from recall, the simplest thought process, to the most abstract order of thinking, synthesis. A taxonomy is a scale, the use of which is a means of establishing where along a hierarchy of thinking one is operating. The point of the test questions is to build a series of test items that incorporate the range of thinking skills as they are reflected in the Taxonomy.

Item 1. Knowledge of specific facts. The answers here must be selected from a group of possibilities. The correct answer selected from multiple alternatives is a directly stated fact in the story. This retention skill would correspond to Bloom's knowledge category, especially to "Knowledge of Specific Facts." The nature of the articles, of course, contributes to the awareness of facts about particular cultures, etc.

Item 2. Recognition of meaning of word in context. The student must choose and write the correct response. This skill corresponds to Bloom's "Knowledge of Terminology," especially to the area of "Familiarity with a large number of words in their common range of meaning."

Item 3. This item is intended to make pupils aware of correct form and usage. The student must select the word, or words, described by the words used in the stem of the question. It may be an adjective, a descriptive phrase, or even the predicate of the sentence. The student must find the necessary word in the story and write it. This skill falls within Bloom's "Knowledge of Conventions."

Item 4. Recognition of implications or inferences. This item requires selecting the correct inference from several choices. The response required comes from a multiple choice of implied details. The skill relates to Bloom's "Extrapolation."

Item 5. Knowledge of specific facts and retention of details. This item requires the reader to select the correct answer from a group of possibilities. See *Item 1* above. This skill requires attention to the task of reading.

Item 6. Recognition of the meaning of the whole. This item requires the reader to select the answer which best describes the central theme of the story. This skill corresponds to Bloom's "Meaning of the Whole Interpretation."

Item 7. Recognition of implications or inferences. This item requires selecting the correct inference from several choices. The response required comes from a multiple choice of implied details. The skill relates to Bloom's "Extrapolation."

Item 8. The item expects the learner to make an interpretation. The reader must confirm an understanding of the nature of a fact, process, or problem. He must select the one response among the given alternatives which most nearly shows the cause, or the meaning, of the stated effect as explained in the story. This item corresponds to Bloom's level two of thinking: "Comprehension."

Item 9. The question falls within Bloom's category of "synthesis." The entire activity of associating the information in individual articles with an overriding concept requires a synthesis of ideas. The last skills question lets the pupil select a clear statement about the way in which the article points toward the larger concept.

In order to select the correct alternative, the student must reject irrelevant ideas and put together facts and reasonable implications which tend to support the given concept.

Method

Each story has been written to the specifications for a controlled vocabulary and readability level. The readability level of this book was determined through application of the Dale-Chall Readability Formula. See the manual for statistical information.

Words not in the controlled vocabulary list were limited to words according to standard lists of words suitable for pupils slightly older than their reading level would imply. In some cases, the content required the use of a highly specialized word. Such words are carefully defined by context clues in the story itself and are listed in the index.

Field Testing

In the testing population, a wide range of background and abilities of pupils were represented. See the manual for details. The results of extensive field testing were used to revise the materials until an optimum ease index was achieved. Preliminary practice should be provided. See "Steps for the Reader" before the opening selection for specific directions.

The teacher should also remind the pupil where it is necessary to look back into the story to find answers.

Concept Recapitulations

After pupils have completed the text, the following suggestions may be helpful in conducting a discussion which will tie together the information carried in the individual articles in terms of the overall concept. This type of activity is important not for the particular information pupils will meet in these books but for the beginnings of building a wider view of the human environment. Information from widely divergent fields can interact to contribute to broad, intellectual awareness, whereas most education tends to fracture rather than serve the development of such wide-angle perspective.

Often, those youngsters most resistant to formal educational processing have drawn their own conclusions about the world and how it works. These students, in particular, may take fresh challenge from the experience of using pieces of information as the flexible building blocks for at least one unified meaningful whole. Here skill building in reading has been attached not only to immediate short-range motivation and information accumulation but also to long-range creative reassessment of apparently dissimilar content. Great openness

and considerable flexibility will be required from teachers who will make the greatest use of this aspect of this reading program. The possibilities for student growth and awakenings are enormous.

A procedure such as the following is suggested:

"You have read stories about four big ideas. The first idea was that *change may produce unexpected results*. In the beginning of the book you were asked to keep certain questions in mind. Can you answer these questions now?" (Pupils meet guiding questions on page 13.)

1. Can you always predict what results will occur from a particular change?

2. What kinds of unexpected things happened?

3. Do unexpected results sometimes have great value?

4. How could we be on the look-out for unexpected results?

5. How have unexpected findings been useful?

"The second big idea that you read about was that *some changes are planned; others are accidental*. Can you answer the following questions?" (Guide questions are on page 57.)

1. What are some changes that were planned?

2. What are some accidental changes that have taken place?

3. Do accidental changes ever create greater results than planned ones?

4. When do you suppose change is good for people? When is it not good?

5. Do people adjust to change easily? Why or why not?

"The third big idea is *modern ways of life require planned change*. Can you answer the following questions?" (Guide questions are on page 101.)

1. How has our country benefited from planned change?

2. What kinds of changes have affected you?

3. Which changes have seemed good?

4. Can you bring about change by yourself?

5. What must a person do to effect change?

"The fourth big idea that you read about was *where might change take us?* Can you answer the following questions?" (Guide questions are on page 145.)

1. What recent changes have affected us?

2. Can you guess what may be the results of a recent change?

3. How will you change because of a particular thing that has happened to you?

4. Have your ideas about change changed?

5. What changes would you like to see? Will you be able to do something about them as an adult?

Have a few priming possibilities ready to suggest, or shape them out of the early offerings from the group. Sophisticated statements and a review of specifics are not necessarily expected. Look for signs of mental play and the movement of information from one setting to another. It is perfectly reasonable to conclude with unanswered questions for pupils to ponder in retrospect. However, it is important to give pupils the satisfaction of enthusiastic acceptance of their early attempts at this type of open-ended speculation.

STEPS FOR THE READER

A. Turn to page 14. Look at the picture. Read the title. Think about what the story will say.

B. Study the words for this page on the list beginning page 188.

C. Read the story carefully.

D. Put your name and the title of the story on a sheet of paper. Number from one to nine. Begin the test on the page next to the story.

1. This question asks you to remember something the story has told you. Which of the four choices will make the sentence say what the story does? Choose that statement.

2. This question asks you to find the word in the story that means the same as the words in slanting type. When the question gives you a paragraph number, read that part again to be sure you have the right word.

3. Reread the paragraph given. Which word is described by the words given in the question? The given words must modify or explain the word or words you select.

4. This question wants you to think about the story. The answer is not in your book. Read the choices. Choose the sentence that is the very best guess you might make from the ideas you have read in the story.

5. The question tests your memory for a detail. Which of the choices agrees with the story?

6. This question asks you to choose a statement about the entire story. Don't select an idea that fits only one small part. Your answer should fit all of the story.

7. On the basis of the story, which of the choices is most likely to be true? The answer is not in the story. You will have to think about the ideas and draw your own conclusions.

8. Question 8 asks why. You must select the best explanation from those listed. The cause should be the one given in the article.

9. Question 9 asks you to think about the article ideas in relation to the concept for the group of articles. The statement you select must be true for the article. It should also be a good illustration of the concept in action.

E. Check your work. The answers for the first test are on page 12. Your teacher may let you use the answer key for other tests. She may check your work for you.

F. Put the number correct at the top of your paper. Now go back and re-check the answers that were wrong. Do you see now how the correct answer was better? How can you get ready to do the next test better?

G. Turn to page 186. The directions tell you how to put your score onto a record chart. Your teacher will tell you if you may write in the book. If not, she will help you make a copy for your notebook.

Looking for the Big Idea

The next page asks questions about the big ideas in this book. Read the page and think about the ideas.

Just for Fun

Your book has three longer stories that are just for fun. These stories, beginning on pages 54, 98, and 142, are from old folktales. There are no questions to answer.

Answers for Practice Test, page 15		
1. c	2. hemisphere	3. Ann Eckels Bailie
4. a	5. b	6. b
7. a	8. b	9. b

I

Change May Produce Unexpected Results

In this section you will read about surprising effects from certain changes. You will read about these things in the areas of history, space, biology, anthropology, economics, geography, earth science, mathematics, engineering, and art.

Keep these questions in mind when you are reading.

1. Do you always get the result that you have worked for?

2. What are some things that have happened that were not intended?

3. Were these unexpected results always good for people?

4. What should be our attitude toward unexpected results?

5. What can be done with unexpected findings?

Shaped Like a Pear

Sailors long ago were often afraid that if they sailed too far from home they would fall off the edge of the flat ocean. In the past, many people had to trust the word of others, for they had no way to gather information for themselves.

Today, we can fly in airplanes high over the earth and see the curve that is proof of its roundness. Astronauts soaring miles high can send us pictures that support our beliefs. Most people now accept the fact that the earth is definitely not flat. But many of them don't realize that it's not exactly round either. Actually, some scientists in the 1950s discovered that the earth is shaped more like a pear, thicker on one end than the other.

A mathematician, Ann Eckels Bailie, used computers to gather information to use in planning space flights. In her work, she figured the distance of spacecraft from the planets and stars.

During her regular work of tracking the second U.S. satellite, Vanguard I, she discovered some facts that didn't seem to make sense. It appeared that the perigee—or point nearest to the earth—of the Vanguard orbit measured a different distance from the northern hemisphere of our earth than from the southern hemisphere.

At first, she and her colleagues thought that the strange figures were due to some mathematical error. But Bailie wouldn't give up the idea that important new information had been discovered. She and the other scientists discussed the shape of the earth again and again. One person even used Silly Putty to show how the earth bulged a little at the equator. Suddenly, Bailie and the others began to see that the same kind of gravitational pull that made the middle bulge might explain the different measurements for the northern and southern hemispheres.

Further research finally supported these beliefs. Bailie's accidental finding gave us a surprising new picture of the shape of the earth.

1. Sailors long ago thought the ocean was
   a. a pear.   c. flat.
   b. round.   d. high.

2. The word in paragraph 5 that means *half of the earth* is _____.

3. The words "a mathematician" in paragraph 3 describe

   _____.

4. While it is not directly stated, the article suggests that
   a. people change their ideas slowly.
   b. more airplanes are needed in science.
   c. people love to change their minds.

5. The perigee is that point in an orbit that is nearest the
   a. satellite.
   b. earth.
   c. computer.

6. On the whole, the article tells about
   a. how most mathematicians work.
   b. an accidental discovery about the earth's shape.
   c. how to track an orbit.

7. Which statement does this article lead you to believe?
   a. Small discoveries can lead to big changes in thought.
   b. Small discoveries aren't worth checking.
   c. Computers aren't much use anymore.

8. Why did Ann Eckels Bailie use computers?
   a. To prove the earth was round.
   b. To gather information for planning space flights.
   c. Because all spacecraft had to carry computers.

9. Think about the concept for this article. Which statement seems true both for the article and for the concept?
   a. Scientists like space study more than mathematics.
   b. New facts can bring about changes in our beliefs.
   c. New facts don't really change old ideas.

Wise Words

In 1833, Lydia Francis Child put into writing her thoughts about slavery. Her book had a long title: *An Appeal in Favor of the Class of Americans called Africans.* Child knew she was taking a chance, but she didn't expect the angry response she received.

Her friends didn't approve; many people stopped talking to her. She had begun to publish *Juvenile Miscellany*, the first magazine for children, but she had to stop publication because so many people had stopped buying the magazine in protest.

Other unexpected things happened, though, that turned out to be good. Some people started thinking about her words. Others decided to free their slaves after reading her words. Famous writers of the time wrote about her bravery in speaking out.

Lydia Francis Child continued to write and publish antislavery journals. She became the editor for an antislavery journal in New York called *The Standard.*

Through this journal, she influenced many thinkers of the times.

Throughout the 1900s, black people began to publish their own writings more and more. Black newspapers began as more writers took advantage of the printed word to put forth their own points of view. Some journals loudly demanded fairness for black citizens.

Today, many black newspapers help black Americans in practical ways. *The Los Angeles Sentinel*, published by Ruth Washington, has become a leader in the black community in the area of real estate and classified ads.

When Ruth Washington took over her business, she didn't know much about publishing. Now she knows how important a newspaper can be to a community. Today, hundreds of these journals for business and general news are published throughout the United States.

1. Lydia Francis Child published the first
   a. slave book.   c. African book.
   b. want ads.   d. children's magazine.

2. The word in paragraph 6 that means *useful* is _____.

3. The words "for business and general news" in the last paragraph refer to

   _____.

4. While it is not directly stated, the article suggests that
   a. people need to learn more about writing.
   b. black Americans publish all community journals.
   c. people can stop a business by not supporting it.

5. Some people thought Lydia Francis Child was too
   a. bold.
   b. young.
   c. tired.

6. On the whole, the article tells about
   a. the way children learn to write.
   b. how to start a newspaper business.
   c. the effects of the printed word on people's thinking.

7. Which statement does this article lead you to believe?
   a. Newspapers don't help communities anymore.
   b. Newspapers are better than books.
   c. Newspapers have supported worthy causes.

8. Why did black writers want to publish their own writings?
   a. Washington passed a law for writers.
   b. They couldn't get any other jobs.
   c. They wanted to write about their own points of view.

9. Think about the concept for this group of articles. Which statement seems true both for the article and for the concept?
   a. Sticking to an idea may have surprising results.
   b. People should quit if their ideas don't work.
   c. Young people are the best writers of new ideas.

Four Clues from Jupiter

In A.D. 150, the Greek astronomer Ptolemy (tol′ə mē) stated that the sun, moon, planets, and stars all orbited the earth, which stood still. For about 1500 years, people accepted Ptolemy's theory. A Polish astronomer named Copernicus (kō pėr′nə kəs) had said that the sun, not the earth, was the center of the solar system. But almost everyone had ridiculed Copernicus.

In 1608, shortly after the telescope was invented, the Italian mathematician Galileo (gal′ə lē′ō) built a powerful telescope for his own use. What miracles he saw when he turned his instrument toward the night sky! For the first time, he saw the moon's craters, mountains, and plains. Scanning the vast sky, he saw thousands of stars no one had ever glimpsed before. Then Galileo observed something that contradicted Ptolemy's entire theory about the solar system.

On a cold January night in 1610, Galileo aimed his telescope at the planet Jupiter. He noticed three little stars near the red planet. When he looked the next night, the little stars had changed position. Then, a fourth star appeared. After that, Galileo kept accurate records of the changing positions of the four stars.

Galileo eventually realized that the "little stars" were not stars at all, but satellites in orbit around Jupiter. He decided then that the earth's moon must be orbiting the earth just as Jupiter's satellites orbited Jupiter. Then he began to believe that all the planets, with their orbiting satellites, were in orbit around the sun. Copernicus had been right, after all.

Galileo was soon in trouble with his church and other leaders of European thought. He had to stand trial for teaching false beliefs, and he was placed under house arrest. But his careful records of the little stars' changing positions around Jupiter had unexpectedly confirmed Copernicus' theory and helped correct people's ideas about the solar system.

1. Galileo was an Italian
    - a. mathematician.
    - b. pediatrician.
    - c. optician.
    - d. magician.

2. The word in paragraph 1 that means *made fun of* is _____.

3. The words "no one had ever glimpsed before" in paragraph 2 refer to the thousands of _____.

4. While it is not directly stated, the article suggests that
    - a. Galileo was a fine astronomer.
    - b. the Greek astronomer was right.
    - c. Copernicus was a Spanish writer.

5. Galileo aimed his telescope at the planet
    - a. Jupiter.
    - b. Mercury.
    - c. Venus.

6. On the whole, the article tells about
    - a. keeping accurate records in space.
    - b. Galileo's important discovery.
    - c. satellites that orbit the moon.

7. Which statement does this article lead you to believe?
    - a. No planet can have more than four satellites.
    - b. Galileo was the discoverer of Jupiter's satellites.
    - c. Jupiter orbits its four satellites.

8. Why did Galileo have to stand trial?
    - a. He was accused of fighting with Copernicus.
    - b. He was accused of keeping accurate records.
    - c. He was accused of teaching false beliefs.

9. Think about the concept for this group of articles. Which statement seems true both for the article and for the concept?
    - a. One person's curiosity changed the thinking of 1500 years.
    - b. One person cannot contradict a theory accepted for centuries.
    - c. People should never question statements by ancient scientists.

Seeing from Space

The astronauts who flew around the earth as a part of Project Mercury were explorers entering a new world. Their reports added to our knowledge of how the human body functions outside the earth's gravity. Some of the other things the astronauts reported were very surprising.

For example, scientists were astonished to learn how clearly the astronauts could see things on earth from 100 miles away.

"I saw several houses with smoke coming from the chimneys in the high country around the Himalayas," Gordon Cooper reported after the *Mercury-Atlas 9* flight of May 1963. Cooper reported seeing a train and the wake of a boat. He also thought he saw a truck moving along a highway.

Photographs were taken from Cooper's capsule. They were clearer than photos taken from high-flying airplanes. This may have been due to the astronaut's cameras being so far away from the air turbulence and dust that cause distortion in photos taken from high-flying airplanes.

Scientists set up vision tests for later astronauts. Certain patterns of white markers were placed on the ground in Texas and Australia. The patterns were kept secret from the astronauts. Yet they easily located the markers and correctly described the patterns.

Today, some scientists think that the earth's gravity may hinder the working of the human eye. For example, on earth gravity may be pulling the soft lens of our eyes out of shape. When the pull of gravity is absent, the soft lens may take on a better shape for seeing clearly. The natural movements of the eye, which help it to see more clearly, may be more effective when a person is "weightless." Whatever the reasons may be for seeing better in space, we are learning new and surprising facts about human vision. The new knowledge is an unplanned result of the space exploration program.

1. Astronauts could see things on earth from
     a. 100 miles away.
     b. high-flying planes.
     c. the Himalayas.
     d. trains and boats.

2. The word in paragraph 4 that means *roughness* or *violence* in the air is

   _____ .

3. The words "with smoke coming from the chimneys" in paragraph 3 describe

   several _____ .

4. While it is not directly stated, the article suggests that
     a. people may learn many surprising things about themselves in space.
     b. space exploration cannot change our knowledge of ourselves.
     c. astronauts have better vision than any other human beings.

5. Certain patterns of white markers were placed on the ground in
     a. Trenton and Alaska.
     b. Tampa and Austria.
     c. Texas and Australia.

6. On the whole, the article tells about
     a. the working of the human eye in space.
     b. natural flickering movements of eyes.
     c. markers and patterns placed on the ground.

7. Which statement does this article lead you to believe?
     a. People are learning new things about the effects of gravity.
     b. Our eyes hurt because gravity is pulling them out of shape.
     c. It is not natural for astronauts to have eyes with soft lenses.

8. Why do we think that the photos were clearer from the capsule than high-flying planes?
     a. Astronauts were given much more expensive cameras.
     b. Air turbulence and dust caused distortion in photos taken in planes.
     c. Cameras do not shake as much in capsules as they do in high planes.

9. Think about the concept for this group of articles. Which statement seems true both for the article and for the concept?
     a. New knowledge is not always the result of planning.
     b. Space experts know everything about man in space.
     c. Earth's gravity only hinders the astronauts.

The Rabbit Invasion

In most parts of the world, rabbits have long been valued for their meat and pelts. Europe has had wild rabbits since the Ice Ages. During the twelfth century, Norman invaders brought European rabbits to England, where the rabbits flourished.

Australia had no rabbits until 1859. Then, an Australian landowner had twenty-four European rabbits sent to him from England. The rabbits multiplied. Four years later, the landowner said that he had killed about 20,000 of them for their meat and pelts. By 1930, the remaining rabbits had multiplied so fast that millions of them had spread over most of Australia.

The rabbits fed on the same grass that nourished Australia's domestic sheep and cattle. The bunnies ate the roots of the grass and chewed off almost every other growing plant they could reach. There was a sharp drop in the number of sheep that an acre of grazing land could feed.

One result of the rabbit invasion was a serious slump in the production of wool, Australia's leading export. And since the rabbit invasion had left the land almost bare of plants, nothing was left to hold down the fertile topsoil. Erosion by wind or water scattered the topsoil and changed once-productive land into useless, desert-like areas.

To solve its rabbit problem, Australia tried bounties, guns, fences, traps, poisons, cats, dogs, and foxes. But it has been myxomatosis (mik sō′ mə tō′ səs), a rabbit disease spread by mosquitoes and rabbit fleas, that finally killed most rabbits. In 1950, the disease killed over 90 percent of Australia's rabbits. Three years later, many of the remaining rabbits had developed an immunity to myxomatosis. Today, Australia's rabbits are still a serious problem.

Although rabbit pelts bring Australia millions of dollars yearly, the money gained is only a small part of the money lost in wool, cattle, and farm crops.

1. Europe has had wild rabbits since the
   - a. Rainy Days.
   - b. Ice Ages.
   - c. Stone Age.
   - d. Bronze Age.

2. The word in paragraph 5 that means *a resistance to a disease* is

   _____ .

3. The words "into useless, desert-like areas" in paragraph 4 describe the

   once-productive _____ .

4. While it is not directly stated, the article suggests that
   - a. certain animals can destroy the land.
   - b. rabbits have been good for Australia.
   - c. wool is produced from the fur of rabbits.

5. Myxomatosis is a rabbit disease spread by
   - a. cats, dogs, and sheep.
   - b. mosquitoes and fleas.
   - c. poisons.

6. On the whole, the article tells about
   - a. Norman invaders who sent rabbits to Australia.
   - b. the effect of the rabbit invasion on Australia.
   - c. changing desert lands into productive topsoil.

7. Which statement does this article lead you to believe?
   - a. Australia's rabbits are no longer a serious problem these days.
   - b. Australia's economy has been affected by the rabbit invasion.
   - c. Australia doesn't need money from wool, cattle, or farm crops.

8. Why doesn't myxomatosis still kill Australian rabbits?
   - a. Many rabbits have developed an immunity to it.
   - b. Myxomatosis only works on cats, dogs, and foxes.
   - c. Australians want to keep the rabbits alive.

9. Think about the concept for this group of articles. Which statement seems true both for the article and for the concept?
   - a. There was a sharp drop in wool because the rabbits ate the sheep.
   - b. Millions of rabbits spread over most of Asia and Africa in 1950.
   - c. The rabbit invasion was not foreseen by the Australian landowner.

each year. Additional millions are lost each year to the appetites of other plant-eating insects. Some of these are corn borers, gypsy moths, potato beetles, and Japanese beetles.

In modern times, many powerful insecticides have been used in an attempt to destroy insects that damage crops and trees. Some kinds of insecticides, when carefully used, have worked well. Yet the same insecticides have caused some unexpected problems. In one large area, an insecticide was used against Japanese beetles, which eat almost any kind of flower or leaf. Shortly afterward, the number of corn borers almost doubled. As intended, the insecticide had killed many Japanese beetles. But it had killed many of the insect enemies of the corn borer as well.

In another case, an insecticide was used in Louisiana to kill the troublesome fire ant. The insecticide did not kill many fire ants. It did kill several small animals. It also killed some insect enemies of the sugarcane borer, a much more destructive pest than the fire ant. As a result, the number of sugarcane borers increased and severely damaged the sugarcane crop.

To be sure that one insect pest will not be traded for another when an insecticide is used, scientists must perform careful experiments and do wide research. The experiments and research provide knowledge of the possible hazards an insecticide may bring to plant and animal communities. Without such knowledge, we have found that nature sometimes responds to insecticides in unexpected ways.

Nature's Revenge

For as long as humans have raised crops as a source of food and other products, insects have damaged them. Between 1870 and 1880, locusts ate millions of dollars worth of crops in the Mississippi Valley. Today in the United States the cotton boll weevil damages about 300 million dollars worth of crops

1. An insecticide was used in Louisiana to kill the troublesome
   - a. lady bug.
   - b. butterfly.
   - c. firefly.
   - d. fire ant.

2. The word in the last paragraph that means *dangers* is _____.

3. The words "a much more destructive pest" in paragraph 3 describe the

   _____ _____.

4. While it is not directly stated, the article suggests that
   - a. insecticides are not dangerous to any small animals.
   - b. insecticides do not always accomplish their purpose.
   - c. insecticides are no longer being used to kill insects.

5. Locusts ate millions of dollars worth of crops in the
   - a. Great Smoky Mountains.
   - b. Mishawaka Delta.
   - c. Mississippi Valley.

6. On the whole, the article tells about
   - a. the appetites of plant-eating bugs.
   - b. the best way to kill boll weevils.
   - c. the dangers in using insecticides.

7. Which statement does this article lead you to believe?
   - a. All changes are predictable.
   - b. Nothing ever changes in nature.
   - c. Nature is not always predictable.

8. Why must scientists perform careful experiments and do wide research?
   - a. They must learn to destroy all the insects that we need.
   - b. They must be sure one insect pest is not traded for another.
   - c. Research keeps them from inventing new insecticides for the crops.

9. Think about the concept for this group of articles. Which statement seems true both for the article and for the concept?
   - a. Insects that destroy crops should be kept alive.
   - b. Insecticides were not meant to kill off insect enemies.
   - c. Insect enemies are not important to crop growing.

The Help That Failed

The General Allotment Act, passed in 1887 by the United States Congress, was expected to help the American Indians. The act called for breaking up tribal reservations and turning them into family-sized farms. Each farm would be given to an individual Indian.

The government thought that the Indians would be better off if they forgot their tribal organizations and their tribal languages. The government thought that Indians who owned land and farmed for a living would become more like other Americans.

But it didn't work out that way. The Indians were used to living in tribal groups, and sharing with each other. They had always thought of land as something that belonged to the whole tribe, rather than to individuals.

With their families scattered on separate farms, many Indians were dissatisfied. The land they were given was often poor, and they hadn't the skill to farm it well. Poverty and poor health increased, and the Indians clung to their old languages and customs.

Eventually the government realized that the division of reservation land had made things worse rather than better for the Indians.

The Indian Reorganization Act, passed in 1934, reversed the government's policy. This act said that all Indian land should be owned by tribes, rather than by individuals. The new act encouraged tribal organizations to take responsibility for running Indian affairs. The act also provided money which tribes could borrow to buy more land or to start businesses.

Soon Indian tribes were running motels, factories, and cattle ranches. Some tribes reorganized as corporations. With help from government agencies, many tribes improved their housing, health care, and schools.

Although there is still poverty and ill health on the reservations, there is also hope that better days lie ahead.

FIND THE ANSWERS

1. The General Allotment Act was expected to help the American
   - a. Mexicans.
   - b. Indians.
   - c. Southerners.
   - d. Spaniards.

2. The word in paragraph 4 that means *held fast* is _____.

3. The words "something that belonged to the whole tribe" in paragraph 3 describe the _____.

4. While it is not directly stated, the article suggests that
   - a. Americans who own land and farm it are Indians.
   - b. Indians were used to living like the settlers.
   - c. the settlers did not understand Indian ways.

5. The government's policy was reversed by the
   - a. Indian Reconstruction Bill.
   - b. Indian Reorganization Act.
   - c. Indian Allotment Program.

6. On the whole, the article tells about
   - a. the good land that was given to Indians.
   - b. tribal organizations and tribal acts.
   - c. helping Indians on the reservations.

7. Which statement does this article lead you to believe?
   - a. The government wanted to break up family farms.
   - b. It is not always easy to give up old customs.
   - c. New customs are always better than old ones.

8. Why did the government want Indians to own land and farm for a living?
   - a. It thought this would make the Indians more like other Americans.
   - b. It wanted to see if individual Indians would drop out of school.
   - c. It wanted to see if matters could become worse on the reservation.

9. Think about the concept for this group of articles. Which statement seems true both for the article and for the concept?
   - a. A planned change may not always produce the expected results.
   - b. The government encouraged the Indians to drop responsibility.
   - c. Indians cannot plan to run motels, factories, or cattle ranches.

The highest castes were the Brahmins, who were priests and scholars forbidden to work with their hands. Below them, like rungs in a ladder, were soldiers, merchants, farmers, and laborers. So low as to be almost completely outside the caste system were the untouchables. These people could not live inside the villages, drink water from public wells, or walk on public roads.

In 1947, when India became an independent democracy, a law was passed abolishing untouchability. Today, other laws are being more effective in breaking down the caste barriers.

Land reform is one such law. Today in India, a person may own only a certain amount of land and must use all land owned. As a result, Brahmins are no longer idle landowners collecting rents from large estates. They manage their own small farms; some even plant and harvest crops with their own hands.

In 1950, every adult in India was given the right to vote. Since then, very few Brahmins have been elected to high office because the Brahmins make up such a small caste. The middle castes and untouchables hold more voting power than the Brahmins.

In India, as in most parts of the world, people are flocking to cities to live. By living in crowded apartments, sharing public transportation, and working side by side in factories, different castes cannot avoid contact with each other. In India's crowded cities, some caste distinctions are being forgotten.

Slowly but surely, new forces at work in India are unexpectedly doing more to break down the caste system than the 1947 law which abolished untouchability.

Democracy Comes to India

For centuries, social barriers and religious laws have separated the Hindus of India into class groups called castes. Each caste did only certain work and lived in a certain way. Each caste avoided contact with a lower caste.

FIND THE ANSWERS

1. The highest castes in India were the
    - a. Builders.
    - b. Bankers.
    - c. Brahmins.
    - d. Burmese.

2. The word in paragraph 6 that means *differences* is

    _____ .

3. The words "living in crowded apartments" in paragraph 6 tell about the

    different _____ .

4. While it is not directly stated, the article suggests that
    - a. priests and scholars were untouchable.
    - b. the untouchables led miserable lives.
    - c. all untouchables were rich people.

5. Every adult in India was given the right to vote in
    - a. 1509.
    - b. 1590.
    - c. 1950.

6. On the whole, the article tells about
    - a. the caste system in India.
    - b. sharing transportation.
    - c. drinking from public wells.

7. Which statement does this article lead you to believe?
    - a. Brahmins are leaving India to start a caste system here.
    - b. The caste system has lost its importance in India.
    - c. Every country should have a caste system like India's.

8. Why have very few Brahmins been elected to high office since 1950?
    - a. The middle castes and untouchables hold more voting power.
    - b. They do not want to serve in high office in a democracy.
    - c. They prefer to spend their time walking on public roads.

9. Think about the concept for this group of articles. Which statement seems true both for the article and for the concept?
    - a. The Brahmins were all soldiers, merchants, and laborers.
    - b. Social barriers were broken down by the force of democracy.
    - c. Brahmins and untouchables have always been close friends.

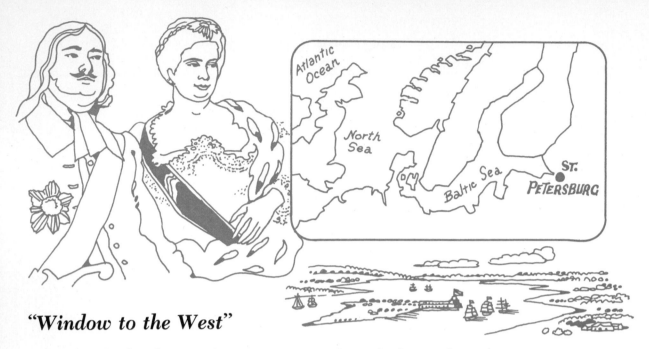

"Window to the West"

For hundreds of years, Russia was a backward nation because it had no good seaport. Czar Peter the Great, who ruled Russia from 1689 to 1725, fought a war with Sweden to gain seaports on the Baltic Sea. He founded a new Baltic seaport, St. Petersburg, now Leningrad, and made it Russia's capital.

Czar Peter's aim was to make Russia a world power by introducing foreign trade. He felt that foreign money could help to develop his country's natural resources and to build up its industry. The new seaport was a "window to the west" that made his plan possible.

When Czar Peter died, Russia was producing more iron than any European country. New factories were busy making supplies for Russia's army. Russia was becoming a world power. But the country was changing in a way that was not part of Czar Peter's plan.

Before Czar Peter's reign, Russia's population was made up of two groups—the serfs who worked on the farms, and the wealthy, landowning nobles. The Czars had complete power over everyone. But now foreign trade and the new industries produced new groups made up of merchants, factory owners, and factory workers. These groups developed interests and demands of their own. Peter and many of the Czars who followed him used their powers ruthlessly to crush all groups that resisted them.

By the late 1800s, most of the Russian people were dissatisfied and angry. The merchants and factory owners were demanding more voice in the government. The serfs, freed in 1861, wanted land, and the factory workers wanted better wages and working conditions.

In 1917, the Russian people revolted. They toppled the hated government of Czar Nicholas II and after several false starts established communism, the form of government that rules Russia today. Czar Peter could not have guessed what far-reaching influences his "window to the west" would have on Russia and its people.

1. Russia was a backward nation because it had no good
   - a. seaport.
   - b. capital.
   - c. windows.
   - d. navy.

2. The word in paragraph 4 that means *showing no mercy or pity* is

   _____ .

3. The words "the form of government that rules Russia today" in the last para-

   graph describe _____ .

4. While it is not directly stated, the article suggests that
   - a. Russia was once a large agricultural nation.
   - b. serfs owned all the land in Russia long ago.
   - c. the wealthy nobles worked the farms themselves.

5. Before Czar Peter's reign, Russia was made up of
   - a. merchants and workers.
   - b. serfs and nobles.
   - c. Czars and Swedes.

6. On the whole, the article tells about
   - a. factory workers who wanted better wages.
   - b. the changes that took place in Russia.
   - c. the weak government of Czar Nicholas II.

7. Which statement does this article lead you to believe?
   - a. The merchants demanded that the Czars have more control over Russia.
   - b. The Russian people were always completely satisfied with the Czars.
   - c. Russia might have remained a monarchy if the Czars had been kinder.

8. Why did the Czars use their powers ruthlessly?
   - a. They wished to change Russia's population.
   - b. They wished to crush all groups resisting them.
   - c. They wanted to give factory workers good wages.

9. Think about the concept for this group of articles. Which statement seems true both for the article and for the concept?
   - a. Czar Peter the Great ruled Sweden from Leningrad.
   - b. Czar Peter's actions began the new trends in Russia.
   - c. Leningrad is the only seaport Russia has ever had.

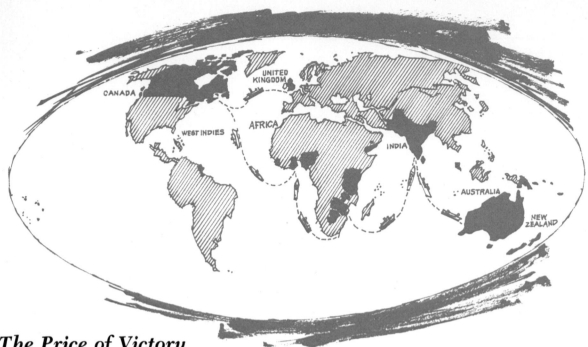

The Price of Victory

One might expect a strong and wealthy nation that wins its wars to become even wealthier and more powerful. Yet Great Britain, which won victories in both world wars, lost most of its overseas empire, much of its wealth, and its position of leadership in the world.

At the beginning of World War I, Great Britain was the richest and strongest nation in the world. The British Navy controlled the seas. The British monarch ruled one-fourth of the world's population. Large amounts of British money were invested throughout the world.

When World War I was over, Great Britain had retained its colonies, but some of them were becoming restless. In Africa and Asia, British colonials had seen their rulers fighting other Europeans. They had lost some of their respect for Great Britain. To pay for the war, Britain had to reclaim money that had been invested overseas.

World War II also cost Great Britain large sums of money. German bombs had damaged English cities and demolished English factories. Forced to fight on several different fronts, the British armed forces could no longer protect all of Great Britain's distant colonies. The Japanese soon occupied certain Asian colonies.

When World War II was over, more colonies in Asia were reluctant to return to British domination. India and the British colonies in Africa demanded self-rule. Granted their independence, these new nations kept a few bonds with Britain as members of the British Commonwealth, but the empire was no longer a great source of wealth.

Britain could no longer afford a great navy. Instead of lending money to other nations, Britain had to borrow money.

Great Britain won its wars, but the price of victory was unexpectedly high.

32

FIND THE ANSWERS

1. Some of Great Britain's colonies in Asia were occupied by the
   a. Portuguese.
   c. Chinese.
   b. Vietnamese.
   d. Japanese.

2. The word in paragraph 2 that means *king or queen* is _____.

3. The words "forced to fight on several different fronts" in paragraph 4 refer to
   the British _____ _____.

4. While it is not directly stated, the article suggests that
   a. Great Britain is as strong as ever.
   b. Great Britain still rules the world.
   c. Great Britain is now a poor country.

5. India and the British colonies in Africa demanded
   a. self-rule.
   b. some bonds.
   c. more money.

6. On the whole, the article tells about
   a. damaged English cities and demolished factories.
   b. the price Great Britain has paid for its wars.
   c. large amounts of money Britain has invested.

7. Which statement does this article lead you to believe?
   a. Great Britain became stronger and wealthier.
   b. Wars are the only way to settle arguments.
   c. Wars can be costly in many different ways.

8. Why did Great Britain have to reclaim much of its money from overseas?
   a. Great Britain needed the money to pay for the war.
   b. Great Britain wanted money to demolish its factories.
   c. Great Britain needed the money to buy German bombs.

9. Think about the concept for this group of articles. Which statement seems true
   both for the article and for the concept?
   a. When World War II was over, Britain was ruled by colonials.
   b. One result of World War II was the creation of new nations.
   c. Very few changes are ever brought about by world wars.

The Farms That Blew Away

By 1865, when the Civil War ended, not much unused farmland was left in the eastern half of the United States. But farther west, on the Great Plains that included the Dakotas and the western parts of Kansas and Nebraska, there was plenty of free land for the taking.

Those who had visited the Great Plains said that the land closely resembled the fertile prairies of Illinois and eastern Kansas. The dark brown soil was thickly blanketed with rich grass. Railroads were being built across the Plains, and settlers would eventually be able to ship farm products from there to eastern markets.

Many settlers migrated west to the Great Plains. They plowed up the deep-rooted wild grasses that had held down the fertile topsoil, and they planted wheat and corn.

The settlers learned, in time, that the Great Plains was not like Illinois or eastern Kansas. For one thing, there was less rainfall; and rainfall varied widely from year to year. Strong winds blew all summer long. In drought years, crops died and the loosened topsoil that was no longer anchored by the roots of the grasses blew away. In good years, when there was better-than-average rainfall, farmers prospered.

Then, in the 1930s, disaster struck. One dry year followed another. Lakes, rivers, and wells went dry. In 1933, people in New York and other eastern cities saw ochre-colored clouds that sometimes obscured the sun. They were dust clouds, and they contained some of the fertile topsoil of the Great Plains.

The settlers who moved to the western plains had not expected to destroy the land they tried to farm. But they nearly transformed it into a desert. They gave to some parts of the Great Plains a new name—the Dust Bowl.

1. The new name given to the Great Plains by the settlers was the
   - a. Sugar Bowl.
   - b. Dirty Bowl.
   - c. Rose Bowl.
   - d. Dust Bowl.

2. The word in paragraph 5 that means *darkened or hid from sight* is

   _____ .

3. The words "that had held down the fertile topsoil" in paragraph 3 describe the

   deep-rooted wild _____ .

4. While it is not directly stated, the article suggests that
   - a. rainfall in the Great Plains is the same all year long.
   - b. the Great Plains might have been saved if used properly.
   - c. it is easy to replace fertile topsoil once it is gone.

5. The Great Plains included the Dakotas and the western parts of
   - a. Kalamazoo and Nome.
   - b. Kansas and Nebraska.
   - c. Kentucky and New York.

6. On the whole, the article tells about
   - a. ochre-colored clouds that were seen in New York.
   - b. the deep-rooted wild grasses in the Dakotas.
   - c. the result of poor farming in the Great Plains.

7. Which statement does this article lead you to believe?
   - a. Crops of wheat and corn grow better in dust than topsoil.
   - b. Many people besides farmers are affected by a crop failure.
   - c. Crops are important only to the people who grow them today.

8. Why did disaster strike in the 1930s?
   - a. Gentle winds blew all winter long.
   - b. There was too much of a rainfall.
   - c. One dry year followed another.

9. Think about the concept for this group of articles. Which statement seems true both for the article and for the concept?
   - a. The settlers didn't realize how their farming would affect the land.
   - b. The farmers learned that the Great Plains were like eastern Kansas.
   - c. The farmers prospered when ochre-colored clouds obscured the sun.

Of Time and the Railroads

Those who planned and constructed the first American railroads were people of great vision. They predicted that their "iron horses" would open vast expanses of land to farming and industry. They knew that towns would spring up along the new railroads. Yet few of these pioneers could have guessed that American railroads would establish the system of time used throughout most of the world today.

Until the 1880s, all time in the United States was sun time. Farmers set their clocks to noon when the sun appeared to be overhead. In towns, people set their clocks by a courthouse clock or factory whistles. One town's time was often different from the time in a neighboring town.

As the new railroads expanded, large numbers of people began to travel. But the railroads were unable to print accurate timetables when most towns along their tracks had their clocks set differently. There was need for a change, and the railroads led in planning it.

In 1883, railroads in the United States and Canada adopted standard time, a system that divided the continent into four time zones. Within each zone, all railroad clocks were set to an identical time. When it was noon in the Eastern Zone, it was eleven o'clock in the Central Zone, ten o'clock in the Mountain Zone, and nine o'clock in the Pacific Zone. Railroad time signals were sent out by the newly invented telegraph.

Standard time quickly spread. Traveling business people set their watches to match the railroad clocks. Factories and schools followed the railroad's lead. Soon, nearly everyone in the United States and Canada was using the four-zone time system — standard time.

Today, nearly all the world keeps standard time according to an international system of twenty-four time zones.

1. Until the 1880s, all time in the United States was
   a. fun time.   c. spring time.
   b. sun time.   d. moon time.

2. The word in paragraph 5 that means *agree with* is _____.

3. The words "of great vision" in paragraph 1 describe the _____.

4. While it is not directly stated, the article suggests that
   a. farmers set their clocks according to the factory whistles.
   b. the correct time was not too important before the 1800s.
   c. only people who traveled on trains ever knew the time.

5. Railroad time signals were sent out by the newly invented
   a. television.
   b. telephone.
   c. telegraph.

6. On the whole, the article tells about
   a. pioneers who rode on "iron horses."
   b. large numbers of people who traveled.
   c. the establishment of standard time.

7. Which statement does this article lead you to believe?
   a. Accurate timetelling is important to many industries.
   b. Accurate time is important only in the United States.
   c. Accurate time is owned by the people who built railroads.

8. Why weren't railroads able to print accurate timetables?
   a. Towns along the tracks set their clocks differently.
   b. No one was able to read timetables that were accurate.
   c. Farmers preferred to read the sun instead of timetables.

9. Think about the concept for this group of articles. Which statement seems true both for the article and for the concept?
   a. It is much better to run a railroad on courthouse time.
   b. Railroads in Canada refused to accept a standard time system.
   c. The need for standard time zones was not unexpected by early railroad planners.

When the Mississippi Flowed Backward

In 1811, a giant earthquake shook the Mississippi Valley. Although the earthquake did not cause great destruction of property or much loss of life, it may have been the most severe earthquake ever felt in North America.

The quake began late in 1811 as a series of shocks that were most violent near New Madrid, Missouri. There were no large cities in that area. The few settlers lived mostly in log cabins, which resist earthquakes better than most types of houses.

John James Audubon, the naturalist and painter, was riding horseback in Kentucky when he felt, and saw, the land rising and falling around him. "The earth waved like a field of corn before the breeze," he said. Other people as far distant as New Orleans, Boston, and Canada felt the shocks.

The giant earthquake had many unexpected results. At one point along the Mississippi River, high banks fell into the river from both sides of the stream. The water was forced to the center of its channel where it rose so high that it flowed upstream temporarily.

Large areas were elevated and left 5 to 20 feet higher than they had been. Other areas sank and became swamps or lakes. In western Tennessee, the earthquake lowered a forest 20 feet. Water filled the depression and formed a lake. The trees died, but some of their stumps are still standing.

Lake Eulalie just disappeared. The earthquake opened up two cracks in the lake floor, and its water drained away. A few years later, trees grew where the lake had been.

All in all, about a million square miles of land was affected by the giant earthquake of December 16, 1811.

FIND THE ANSWERS

1. In western Tennessee, the earthquake lowered a
   - a. fountain.
   - b. farmer.
   - c. forest.
   - d. flower.

2. The word in paragraph 5 that means *a hollow or lowered area* is

   _____ .

3. The words "which resist earthquakes better than most types of houses" in

   paragraph 2 describe the log _____ .

4. While it is not directly stated, the article suggests that
   - a. an earthquake makes violent and sudden changes in the land.
   - b. earthquakes cannot change the land in any important way.
   - c. the shocks of an earthquake are rarely felt at any distance.

5. A giant earthquake shook the Mississippi Valley in
   - a. 1999.
   - b. 1118.
   - c. 1811.

6. On the whole, the article tells about
   - a. the effects of a giant earthquake.
   - b. a naturalist and painter on a horse.
   - c. two cracks in the floor of a lake.

7. Which statement does this article lead you to believe?
   - a. The land looked very different before 1811.
   - b. The face of the land is always the same.
   - c. Lakes cannot disappear and forests cannot die.

8. Why did Lake Eulalie disappear?
   - a. The earthquake lowered a large number of trees over it.
   - b. Its water drained away through two cracks in the lake floor.
   - c. It was covered by about a million square miles of land.

9. Think about the concept for this group of articles. Which statement seems true
   both for the article and for the concept?
   - a. Rivers can never flow upstream, even briefly.
   - b. Changes in nature cannot always be predicted.
   - c. An earthquake rarely produces unexpected change.

The Now-and-Then Island

The floor of the Pacific Ocean is dotted with volcanoes. Some have erupted so often that they have built up islands of hardened lava. Japan, Hawaii, Guam, and the Aleutians are all islands built by volcanoes.

In 1952 men had a rare opportunity to observe this process of island-building, for in September of that year, scientific instruments on shore indicated that a submerged volcano named Myojin had suddenly become active. A Japanese ship steamed out to investigate Myojin, which lies 250 miles south of Tokyo.

The men on board the ship saw a remarkable sight. Jagged black rocks had formed a new island several hundred feet long. The heat was so great that water around the rocks boiled, while clouds of steam and gas rose high in the air.

A few days later the island disappeared. The cooling rock had formed a plug that sealed the vent of the volcano.

When pressure built up again inside the volcano, new and violent eruptions occurred. The island was torn apart, and the rocks sank beneath the surface of the sea.

A Japanese research ship reached the site on September 24. This ship may have been directly over the volcano when it erupted a third time. A few fragments of the ship were found later. All thirty-one people aboard were lost.

The island appeared once again when new masses of lava were thrown up. For a while, a steep-sided cone of rock rose 300 feet above the sea.

Mapmakers wondered if they should mark Myojin on their charts as an island. Was it there to stay?

A year after the first Japanese ship had visited Myojin, United States ships visited the site, not knowing what to expect. They found only a calm sea. Myojin was quiet again, and the island was gone.

1. Myojin lies 250 miles south of
   a. Tokyo.
   b. Toronto.
   c. Toledo.
   d. Tampico.

2. The word in paragraph 2 that means *sunk under water* is

   _____ .

3. The words "that sealed the vent of the volcano" in paragraph 4 describe a

   _____ .

4. While it is not directly stated, the article suggests that
   a. rocks in the Pacific Ocean are boiled.
   b. some research work may be dangerous.
   c. Japan erupted from a volcano in 1952.

5. The floor of the Pacific Ocean is dotted with
   a. vultures.
   b. volcanoes.
   c. vampires.

6. On the whole, the article tells about
   a. mapmakers who wonder about their charts.
   b. a Japanese research ship in the Pacific.
   c. an island that appeared and disappeared.

7. Which statement does this article lead you to believe?
   a. The land is still changing.
   b. Only Japanese live on islands.
   c. All volcanoes are submerged.

8. Why were only fragments of the Japanese research ship found?
   a. It may have sailed to another area in the Pacific Ocean.
   b. The Japanese scientists took pieces of the ship home.
   c. It may have been over the volcano when it erupted.

9. Think about the concept for this group of articles. Which statement seems true both for the article and for the concept?
   a. Islands may make an unexpected appearance in an ocean.
   b. Volcanoes that are submerged are no longer very active.
   c. Once an island disappears it can never be expected to appear again.

weather forecasters, and space scientists use computers. Businesspeople and engineers use them to keep track of materials and to make out payroll checks.

In many cases, information is fed into the computer by means of cards with holes punched in them. A code determines where and how many holes are punched in a card. In this way, numbers and facts are translated into a language that a computer can read.

Electronic computers have been used since 1946, but the punched cards so important to some of them date as far back as 1728. In that year, a French engineer invented a loom that wove patterns controlled by punched cards. It is usually called the Jacquard loom, after another French designer who made changes to improve it. This loom brought great changes to the textile industry.

The Jacquard loom was the first one that could weave different patterns automatically. The punched cards determined the pattern. When a card was in place on the loom, needles pressed against it. Some needles could pass through holes in the card, and those needles wove the yarn into a certain pattern. Then, another punched card fell into place on the loom and a different pattern resulted.

In the early 1800s, a mathematician, Ada August, Countess of Lovelace, wrote about a remarkable contraption invented by her colleague, Charles Babbage. She described the first scientific use of a computer and previewed the inventions of today.

The early inventors might be surprised to see their punched cards used in so many ways.

The Useful Holes

Modern computers are electronic marvels that store information, recall facts, and work out long, difficult math problems. They are much faster and more accurate than people working with pencils and paper. Mathematicians,

1. Where and how many holes are punched in a card is determined by a
   - a. cold.
   - c. crow.
   - b. clan.
   - d. code.

2. The word in paragraph 3 that means *designs* is _____.

3. The word "they" in paragraph 1 refers to _____.

4. While it is not directly stated, the article suggests that
   - a. people can work problems more accurately than computers.
   - b. many industries could not do without computers today.
   - c. mathematicians are the only people who need computers.

5. The Jacquard loom was invented by a
   - a. Belgian.
   - b. Dutch person.
   - c. French person.

6. On the whole, the article tells about
   - a. early beginnings and present-day use of computers.
   - b. punching cards to fall into place on weaving looms.
   - c. translating numbers and facts on looms for computers.

7. Which statement does this article lead you to believe?
   - a. It is not possible to use a loom to weave patterns by computer.
   - b. Punched cards should never have been invented by the textile industry.
   - c. Old ideas influence many modern inventions.

8. Why is one loom called the Jacquard loom?
   - a. It is the only loom that uses yarn and needles electrically.
   - b. It is a special loom made up of miniature copper brushes.
   - c. It is named for the person who redesigned and improved it.

9. Think about the concept for this group of articles. Which statement seems true both for the article and for the concept?
   - a. Designers with pencils work inside modern electronic computers.
   - b. Inventions planned for one industry have often affected others.
   - c. Modern computers are electronic marvels invented by Jacquard.

The Theory That Exploded

In 1902, no one would hire twenty-three-year-old Albert Einstein as a professor of physics, so he took a job as clerk in a Swiss patent office. In his spare time he concentrated on his own scientific theories.

In 1905, three of Einstein's theories were published. One theory dealt with matter and energy. The theory contained a formula that looked very simple: $E = mc^2$. It means that the energy (E) in any amount of matter equals the mass (m) of the matter (the amount of material in the matter) multiplied by the speed of light squared (c^2). It was a short formula, but Einstein developed it through extremely complex mathematics.

Until Einstein's theory of matter and energy was published, scientists believed that matter and energy were different things. Energy was power, or the ability of a system to do work, while matter was anything you could actually weigh.

Einstein's short formula states that matter and energy are just different forms of the same thing. Matter can change into energy, and energy into matter. Einstein showed scientists how to calculate the amount of energy in a known amount of matter. A pound of matter, said Einstein, contains energy enough to send an ocean liner across the Atlantic and back.

Einstein's theory opened up new questions. How could the energy in matter be unlocked? How would this energy be used? Not until 1942 did scientists find a way to unlock the energy in the uranium atom.

The young Einstein who clerked in the Swiss patent office had not expected that his formula would first be put to use in the atomic bombs exploded over Japan in 1945. Speaking of atomic energy, Dr. Einstein later said, "My part in it was quite indirect. I did not, in fact, foresee that it would be released in my time."

FIND THE ANSWERS

1. Scientists first unlocked energy in the uranium
   - a. bomb.
   - b. light.
   - c. atom.
   - d. cell.

2. The word in paragraph 2 that means *very complicated* or *difficult to understand* is _____.

3. The words "who clerked in the Swiss patent office" in the last paragraph describe the young _____.

4. While it is not directly stated, the article suggests that
   - a. scientists knew matter and energy were the same.
   - b. Albert Einstein was a brilliant scientist.
   - c. Einstein's formulas were developed simply.

5. The first atomic bombs were exploded in 1945 over
   - a. Japan.
   - b. China.
   - c. Tibet.

6. On the whole, the article tells about
   - a. scientific theories that are not published.
   - b. Einstein's theory of matter and energy.
   - c. the Swiss patent office and its clerks.

7. Which statement does this article lead you to believe?
   - a. The first atomic bomb was used in a Swiss patent office.
   - b. Einstein knew that atomic energy would be released in his time.
   - c. Einstein didn't want his formula used to make atomic bombs.

8. Why did Einstein take a job as a clerk?
   - a. He thought it would help to see the patents.
   - b. He wanted to work in a shoe store selling shoes.
   - c. No one would hire him as a professor of physics.

9. Think about the concept for this group of articles. Which statement seems true both for the article and for the concept?
   - a. Einstein's theory was completely wrong.
   - b. Einstein's theory was not important.
   - c. Einstein's theory changed our world.

From Planes to Trains?

In 1945, United States railroads carried nearly 900 million passengers. In 1965, they carried a little more than 300 million. During the same twenty years, the number of passengers carried by airlines soared from 7 million to nearly 100 million.

The great upsurge in air travel was largely due to the airplanes developed during and after World War II. Because these new airplanes were larger than prewar planes, they could carry more passengers at lower fares than ever before. And the newer planes were much faster than prewar airliners had been. For example, jet-powered airliners are almost twice as fast as prewar airliners.

But the capacity and speed of the new airliners have created unexpected problems for air travelers. Most jet aircraft require long runways, and some cities have had to relocate their airports far from their downtown areas. As a result, it may take an air traveler a long time to travel to and from an airport.

The increased number of flights scheduled by the airlines has caused air traffic congestion at some large airports. During rush hours, many airlines want to use the same runways at the same time. Some planes have to circle overhead waiting their turns to land. Others must line up on the taxiways waiting their turns to take off.

The United States must solve its air travel problems soon. Otherwise, rail travel may be due for a comeback. Trains are much slower than planes, but they usually depart and arrive on schedule. And they carry their passengers from a downtown station in one city to a downtown station in another city. One of America's largest railroads is already running high-speed passenger trains between New York City and Washington, D.C. In both of these busy cities, airplane traffic jams have caused unexpected delays. The resulting inconvenience affects hundreds of air travelers and the businesses that brought them to the city.

1. Most jet aircraft require long
   - a. runways.
   - b. raceways.
   - c. causeways.
   - d. breakaways.

2. The word in paragraph 3 that means *the power or ability to do something* is

   _____ .

3. The words "soared from 7 million to nearly 100 million" in paragraph 1 describe the number of _____ .

4. While it is not directly stated, the article suggests that
   - a. the best way to travel is by steamboat.
   - b. more people may start using trains again.
   - c. there is no congestion in air traffic.

5. The great upsurge in air travel developed during and after
   - a. the Civil War.
   - b. World War II.
   - c. the War of the Roses.

6. On the whole, the article tells about
   - a. New York City and Washington.
   - b. rush hours in our cities.
   - c. problems in air travel.

7. Which statement does this article lead you to believe?
   - a. During rush hours, many airlines build their own runways.
   - b. An airplane always takes off and lands on schedule.
   - c. Passengers are upset by delays in air travel.

8. Why is there congestion at some large airports?
   - a. Trains bring their passengers directly to large airports.
   - b. Airlines have scheduled an increased number of flights.
   - c. Passengers must all take the same plane at the same time.

9. Think about the concept for this group of articles. Which statement seems true both for the article and for the concept?
   - a. Faster means of travel have created slowdowns in some areas.
   - b. Airports are always in the downtown areas of large cities.
   - c. Trains are much faster than planes when they are on schedule.

Almost Real

Many children and adults have been fascinated by TV series about a bionic man and a bionic woman. These humans had damaged parts of their bodies—an ear, an eye, an arm—replaced with mechanical parts. If you looked inside the bionic arm, instead of muscles you would see wires and tiny electronic tubes! This may seem too much like science fiction. Surely it could never happen in real life!

Actually, bionics is a real science. It brings together knowledge about biology and electronics. Using bionics, scientists can create mechanical things that act like people and animals.

Copying nature is not a new idea. Hundreds of years ago, inventors were making machines that copied animals or flying birds. The idea of bionics is not so much to copy nature as it is to understand how things work in nature.

There are often whole areas of science which study only one animal. Bat research, for instance, tells scientists how bats use their own radar to keep them from crashing into things as they fly about. Radar is needed for all kinds of air travel. Scientists found that the tiny brain of the bat contains better antennae than humans have been able to produce yet.

Another animal on which science keeps its eye is the porpoise. These gentle animals use little clicking noises to make their own kind of sonar, which is the way humans locate underwater objects.

Scientists have copied the special skin of the dolphin, which allows them to move at great speeds. Ships' propellers have even been designed to copy parts of a fish's tail.

The bionic man and woman showed TV audiences at home how artificial parts could work in humans. One day, handicapped people may be helped with mechanical parts that may actually work better than the originals!

1. Bionics is a
    a. kind of bird.
    b. science.
    c. science fiction story.
    d. muscle.

2. The word in paragraph 2 that means *like a machine* is _____.

3. The words "that copied animals or flying birds" in paragraph 3 describe

    _____.

4. While it is not directly stated, the article suggests that
    a. scientists like to appear on TV.
    b. stories on TV could never really happen.
    c. some science fiction stories are based on fact.

5. Radar is something we need in
    a. air travel.
    b. bat study.
    c. TV stories.

6. On the whole, the article tells about
    a. how TV shows are made.
    b. the ways humans have tried to learn from nature.
    c. how to build a mechanical person.

7. Which statement does this article lead you to believe?
    a. New discoveries in science can help the handicapped.
    b. New discoveries help people very little.
    c. The best discoveries occur in bat research.

8. Why do scientists want to study bats?
    a. They use the bats to catch fish.
    b. Bats tell them how tall buildings are.
    c. Bats have an excellent radar system.

9. Think about the concept for this group of articles. Which statement seems true both for the article and for the concept?
    a. We can't learn much new from the world of nature.
    b. Life in nature isn't very interesting to scientists.
    c. Ordinary parts of our world can give us extraordinary discoveries.

From Campfire to Museum

When clay is heated to a certain temperature, a chemical change takes place. The clay becomes hard and water cannot make it soft again.

It was probably an accident that taught prehistoric people to make pottery by firing objects made of clay. Perhaps a piece of dried clay was dropped into a cooking fire. When the ashes cooled, someone picked up the fragment and saw that the clay had changed. It was much harder, and it no longer grew soft when wet. For the people of ancient times, this discovery was very useful. It allowed them to make vessels for carrying and storing liquids.

Even the earliest pottery was usually decorated in some way. The ancient maker of a water jar may have used a pointed stick to scratch zigzag lines on the clay surface before the jar was fired. Sometimes a seashell or a woven mat was used to press patterns into the soft clay. As early as 3000 B.C., potters were painting designs on their jars. They used different kinds of clay mixed with water to produce different colors.

Primitive potters also fired many clay objects that were purely ornamental. In ancient Egypt, potters made clay jewelry. In Babylonia, potters made colored clay tiles to decorate buildings. In South America, potters made religious statues and musical instruments of clay.

Pottery-making is a useful craft that became an art. Although, most of the bowls, jars, and plates used today are made in factories, the making and firing of pottery by hand continues. It is a popular hobby. Professional artists also work with clay. But many of the beautiful vessels made by hobbyists and professional artists are not used for everyday purposes. Instead, they are displayed as art objects in homes and in art museums and galleries.

FIND THE ANSWERS

1. In ancient Egypt, potters made clay
       a. artists.   c. galleries.
       b. crafts.   d. jewelry.

2. The word in paragraph 2 that means *a piece broken off from something* is

   _____ .

3. The words "that were purely ornamental" in paragraph 4 describe the clay

   _____ .

4. While it is not directly stated, the article suggests that
       a. making pottery is an ancient art.
       b. pottery is a modern kind of craft.
       c. only professional artists make pottery.

5. A chemical change takes place in clay when it is
       a. dropped.
       b. heated.
       c. designed.

6. On the whole, the article tells about
       a. the history of pottery-making.
       b. ancient Babylonian decorations.
       c. religious statues in South America.

7. Which statement does this article lead you to believe?
       a. Clay is an ancient substance no longer used.
       b. Clay can be molded easily into many shapes.
       c. Clay is a very difficult material for artists to use.

8. Why is some pottery still made by hand?
       a. It is a popular hobby.
       b. Factories insist upon it.
       c. It is a good way to get rich.

9. Think about the concept for this group of articles. Which statement seems true both for the article and for the concept?
       a. People long ago were against the use of pottery.
       b. It is wrong to make use of an accidental discovery.
       c. Valuable discoveries are sometimes made accidentally.

A New Tool for Artists

Computers are electronic calculators that serve as valuable, timesaving tools for mathematicians, scientists, and engineers. Yet artists have begun to use computers in surprising ways to create new forms of beauty. "Computer art" now hangs in some art galleries, sharing space with conventional paintings and drawings.

Artists use the computer in different ways. One method combines the computer with the oscilloscope. The oscilloscope is an electronic instrument something like a radar screen and something like a TV set. This instrument pictures the changes in an electric current, fed to it by a computer, as points of light on the oscilloscope screen. The artist can program the computer to move the points of light on the screen into the patterns he or she wants. Then he or she photographs the screen. The result may be a delicate, lace-like pattern of scrolls and repeated loops. It can be very beautiful.

Some artists use the computer to change black-and-white photographs into new forms. First, a black-and-white photograph is broken down into tiny squares that are different shades of gray. The computer then converts the squares of each shade into a different symbol, such as a tiny face, star, or animal. The result is a new version of the photograph. When the new version is viewed at close range, only the small symbols are seen clearly. From a distance, however, the viewer sees a shadow-like reproduction of the original photograph.

Some people say that computer art isn't art at all, since it is made by a machine. Others say that since humans made the machine and tell the machine what to do, the result is art, after all. Whatever the truth may be, a basic tool of mathematicians, scientists, and engineers has become an artist's tool as well.

FIND THE ANSWERS

1. Computers are being used in surprising ways by
   - a. engineers.
   - c. astronauts.
   - b. artists.
   - d. aquanauts.

2. The word in paragraph 3 that means *changes* is _____ .

3. The words "sharing space with conventional paintings and drawings" in paragraph 1 refer to "_____ _____."

4. While it is not directly stated, the article suggests that
   - a. museums do not accept photographs.
   - b. computer art is acceptable to all.
   - c. people do not agree about art.

5. One method artists use is to combine computers with
   - a. microscopes.
   - b. telescopes.
   - c. oscilloscopes.

6. On the whole, the article tells about
   - a. using computers as art symbols.
   - b. different shades of gray in art.
   - c. a new electronic form of art.

7. Which statement does this article lead you to believe?
   - a. Art forms change from time to time.
   - b. Conventional paintings are the only art form.
   - c. People will never accept any form of computer art.

8. Why do some people object to the new art?
   - a. They claim the new art is too gray.
   - b. They say there are too many squares.
   - c. They say it is made by a machine.

9. Think about the concept for this group of articles. Which statement seems true both for the article and for the concept?
   - a. Engineers object to having artists use computers in their art.
   - b. Artists are using unusual tools to create new kinds of art.
   - c. Mathematicians and scientists are artists because of computers.

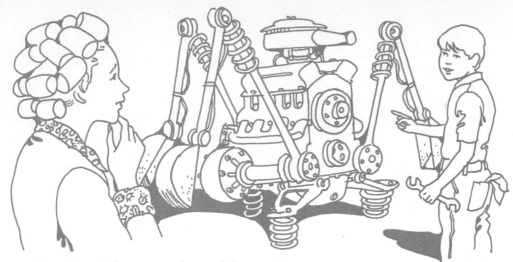

The Remarkable Thermothrockle

Sometimes, when everything is quiet, Harry Heimer goes out into the back yard and stares at the petunia patch. If he listens carefully, he thinks he can hear something rumbling underground. Then Harry has a feeling of real accomplishment. "That old Thermothrockle is still going," he says. "I wonder where it is now."

It all began one day last winter when Harry was in the library. He had asked the librarian for several back issues of *Popular Mechanics Magazine.* Harry was planning to build his own stereo amplifier and was looking for directions.

Tucked into one of the old magazines was a drawing on a wrinkled sheet of paper. It appeared to be of some kind of a mechanical invention.

"What a weird-looking thing," Harry thought. It reminded him of the pictures of those unmanned devices which space scientists had landed on the moon to scoop up samples of soil. It had several hinged arms and legs.

Harry studied the sheet carefully. There seemed to be nothing very difficult about assembling the device. In fact, Harry decided, any boy who had ever tinkered with an Erector set could probably do it.

Harry was puzzled by a note penciled beneath the drawing. It said, "Rejected by U.S. Patent Office as impossible."

Harry might have put the paper back, but he couldn't remember which issue it had been in. It was probably of no value to anyone anyway, Harry told himself. He tucked it into his own notebook and took it home, where he put it in the top drawer of his desk.

Now Harry was not one of those boys who goes out for sports. He never played Little League baseball or entered the annual Golden Gloves tournament. When swimming season came, Harry had other things to do. The "other things" were visits to junk yards. Harry loved junk. His idea of a good time was to take a sandwich and spend the day down at Sam's junk yard. Old Sam was a friend of Harry's and allowed him to come and go as he pleased.

During Harry's frequent visits to Sam's place, he collected various things that he might use in building the invention. He had no idea what the invention was. He had no idea what it would do. For lack of a better name, he referred to it in his own mind as the Thermothrockle. He didn't know what a Thermothrockle was, but the word had a nice solid sound to it.

Each of the parts Harry brought home he put in a pile in the back yard beside the garage. The pile of parts began to grow bigger and bigger. Harry's father threatened to call Sam to come and pick up his junk.

"Just leave it alone, please, Dad," Harry would say. "I'm going to build something."

"Yes, but what?" Mr. Heimer wanted to know.

"Yes, and when?" his mother asked. "You've got the junk lying right over the place where I grow my petunias. It's almost time to plant them."

As spring came on, the pile of junk grew bigger. Mrs. Heimer complained often, but Harry didn't seem to hear.

At last, one Saturday morning in May, Harry had the urge to begin to build. The Thermothrockle went together very easily. When it was about half finished, Harry's old enemy Horace Beeson strolled down the alley. Horace leered at the invention.

"Building a perpetual motion machine, aren't you, Harry?" he said. "I can tell. I've built dozens of them. And I can tell you something else, Harry. They don't work!"

For a moment, Harry was upset. He knew better than to try to build a perpetual motion machine. People had been trying to build perpetual motion machines for centuries. You could read about them in the encyclopedia. They were machines that were supposed to operate forever. They would never run down. Of course, no one had ever succeeded in building one. It was the mark of a real bird-brain—like Horace—to even try such a thing. Since it had never occurred to Harry that his Thermothrockle might be a perpetual motion machine, he ignored Horace.

Mike, down the street, also came to watch. Mike was several years younger than Harry, but he was Harry's friend—always a bit grubby with a runny nose, but a good kid, nevertheless. Sometimes Mike helped Harry, but usually he just sat on the fence and watched. Harry's family did not share Harry's appreciation of Mike. The other Heimers thought Mike was a nuisance and not very bright. He didn't speak plainly and they couldn't understand him.

"What is that thing?" Harry's older sister asked one morning. She had come into the yard to dry her hair in the sun. Harry looked at her head, which was covered with big rollers.

"I haven't told anyone else, Eleanor," he said, "but you might as well know. It's a hair-curling machine."

"You're not very funny, Harry Heimer!" stormed Eleanor. "And I might add that if you spent a little more time on your own appearance, it would be a big improvement."

With one greasy hand, Harry pushed the hair out of his eyes and went on with his work. The Thermothrockle was almost finished. After Eleanor left, Harry bolted the last part into place.

Immediately, the machine began to vibrate. It shook violently and clawed at the ground. Harry was frightened. He quickly unbolted the last part he had attached and the Thermothrockle once again stood motionless.

Harry sat back on his heels to think things over. Perhaps this *was* a perpetual motion machine after all—and a self-starting one, at that. If the Thermothrockle was going to work so well, he wanted to be ready. Perhaps he should have a small ceremony or at least an official observer, someone he could trust.

Harry went to look for Mike. He found him in his kitchen making a sandwich. The small boy followed Harry home.

"Just sit on the fence and watch, Mike," Harry said. "When they test a new airplane, they always have a second pilot in a chase plane watching. Your job is to observe."

"O.K.," said Mike agreeably.

The Thermothrockle was too heavy for Harry to move. It stood near the place where the junk had been—by the garage, in Mrs. Heimer's petunia bed.

"Get ready," said Harry.

"I'm ready," said Mike calmly eating his peanut-butter-and-jelly sandwich. "Do you want a countdown?"

"That's not necessary," said Harry. Gingerly he bolted the final part back into place. At once, there was a whirring and a clanking noise. Mike, startled, fell off the fence backward as the Thermothrockle began to dig. The hinged legs clawed the soil and tossed it into three neat piles. By the time Mike had picked himself up, the Thermothrockle was inside a hole twelve inches deep.

"It's a mechanical mole," Mike announced. "What makes it go?"

"I don't know," said Harry. "And look what it's doing now. It's pulling the dirt into the hole behind it!"

The hinged arms were reaching up to the three piles of dirt. They scooped up the soil and scattered it smoothly over the top of the Thermothrockle. Just before the machine disappeared, one claw reached out and snatched the wrinkled paper on which the plan was drawn.

Mike laughed loudly. "It dug a hole, climbed in, and now it's covered itself up!"

The whirring and clanking machine was out of sight. The earth quivered and shook as the Thermothrockle moved deeper under the petunia bed.

"Maybe I should stop it," said Harry. He ran into the garage for a shovel. He dug frantically for a few minutes then quit. "It's no use, I can't catch up with it."

Just then Harry's mother came into the yard. "Harry," she scolded, "I wish you'd answer when I call you. I've been calling you for five minutes." She paused as she saw Harry with the shovel. "Why how nice, Harry, you've spaded up the flower bed!"

From his perch on the fence, Mike explained. "The Thermothrockle did it."

Mrs. Heimer looked at Mike's jelly-smeared face and shuddered slightly. She wished that boy would clean himself up and learn to speak plainly. She glanced back at the flower bed. For a moment she felt a little dizzy. It looked as if the earth were moving.

"You've even gotten rid of all that junk, Harry. Thank you. This year," she went on, "I think I'll have red petunias."

But Harry wasn't listening. The Thermothrockle had disappeared, taking the plan with it. He knew that he would never be able to build another one.

1246 words

II

Some Changes Are Planned;
Others Are Accidental

In this section you will read about two different ways in which things change. You will read about these things in the areas of history, space, biology, anthropology, economics, geography, earth science, mathematics, engineering, and art.

Keep these questions in mind when you are reading.

1. What are some changes that have been planned?

2. What are some changes that have come by accident?

3. To be good does a change have to be planned?

4. Are people affected by both kinds of change? How?

5. In what ways do you adjust to various changes?

The Long Exile

Israel is a young nation but its people have a long history. The Jews, or Hebrews, first settled on the narrow strip of land at the eastern end of the Mediterranean Sea about 3,500 years ago. They lost this homeland in Roman times and did not get it back again until a few years ago.

Roman soldiers conquered the Jews in 63 B.C., and their land became a Roman province called Judea. Again and again, the Jews rebelled and tried to throw out the conquerors. Finally, in A.D. 132, the Romans ended all resistance by killing many of the Jews and forcing most of the others to leave the country. The Jews who survived were scattered over Europe and Asia. They began a long period of exile.

Wherever they lived, the Jews carefully preserved their religion and laws, their language and customs. They dreamed of their homeland, and planned for the day when they could return to it. They had to wait nearly 2,000 years.

Meanwhile, Arabs, Turks, and European Crusaders warred over the Jewish homeland which came to be known as Palestine. After 1917, Palestine was ruled by Great Britain, though the population was largely Arab. The British allowed Jews to resettle in Palestine if they wished to, and thousands took advantage of this opportunity. The Arabs resented this, and they fought to keep the Jews out. There was constant friction among British, Arabs, and Jews.

Finally, after World War II, Great Britain asked the United Nations to find some solution to the problem. The plan that was adopted, in 1947, called for dividing Palestine into two states, one Arab and the other Jewish. The Arab state became a part of neighboring Jordan. The Jewish state became Israel, the first new nation established under United Nations supervision.

1. The land of Israel was once called
   a. Poland.   c. Persia.
   b. Palestine.   d. Palisades.

2. The word in paragraph 4 that means *rubbing* or *clashing over viewpoint* is

   _____ .

3. The words "a part of neighboring Jordan" in the last paragraph describe the

   _____ _____ .

4. While it is not directly stated, the article suggests that
   a. Arabs and Turks resented the British because they had no religion.
   b. the Jewish religion is one of the world's oldest living religions.
   c. religion did not start until the Crusaders went to Palestine.

5. The province called Judea was ruled by the
   a. Russians.
   b. Romans.
   c. Rumanians.

6. On the whole, the article tells about
   a. the eastern end of the Mediterranean Sea in 1917.
   b. the United Nations after the Second World War.
   c. the history of the Jews and their homeland.

7. Which statement does this article lead you to believe?
   a. People's dreams can survive for centuries.
   b. It is foolish to keep your dreams alive.
   c. A young nation cannot have a long history.

8. Why did the Jews rebel against the Romans?
   a. They wanted to protest against Roman customs.
   b. They wanted to throw out their conquerors.
   c. They wanted to have Turks rule them instead.

9. Think about the concept for this group of articles. Which statement seems true both for the article and for the concept?
   a. The United Nations helped plan the creation of other new nations.
   b. There is no room for any more new nations in the world of today.
   c. Israel is the only new nation the United Nations ever created.

The Luck of Cortez

In 1519, Hernando Cortez marched into central Mexico with an army of 400 men. A year later, this bearded Spaniard and his small force had conquered the mighty Aztec Indian Empire. The Spaniards had superior weapons and they possessed horses, which the Aztecs had never seen before. But that is only part of the story.

Cortez arrived in Mexico during the same year that the Aztecs expected their god Quetzalcoatl (Ket säl′ kwät′ əl) to return. Montezuma, the Aztec ruler, concluded that Cortez was the god Quetzalcoatl. Instead of fighting the Spaniards, the Aztecs welcomed Cortez and his army.

Quetzalcoatl was supposed to have been a human leader of the Aztec people as well as the god they called the Plumed Serpent. In human form, Quetzalcoatl had been a fair-skinned, bearded man who had taught his people such practical skills as farming, building, and metal-working. Then he had sailed away across the eastern sea. Before embarking, he had told the Aztecs he would return in the year 1-Reed. The year that was 1-Reed on the Aztec calendar was 1519 on the European calendar.

Among the messengers who came with gifts of welcome was a young woman, Ce Malinalli. She approached the man the natives believed to be a god. She dressed him in the color black, without telling him that wearing black was the mark of a god. It seems that she had special plans to make Cortez's arrival as magical as possible, without informing him at all. She saw herself as the companion to this conqueror.

She persuaded Cortez not to land as soon as he arrived but to wait until full daylight on the magical day of the year.

Eventually, she traveled at the conqueror's side, as the wise Doña Marina, translating Cortez' every word. After welcoming the strangers, the Aztecs lost 120,000 to 240,000 of their people to the Spaniards. No wonder the natives gave her the name of "princess of suffering."

Cortez was a clever and resourceful soldier, but unplanned circumstances helped him. Because of an accident of history, Cortez the Conqueror was greeted as a god of culture, civilization, and kindness.

1. Quetzalcoatl was a leader of the
   a. Austrians.   c. Aztecs.
   b. Asians.   d. Amazons.

2. The word in paragraph 4 that means *one who wins in war* is _____.

3. The words "a clever and resourceful soldier" in the last paragraph describe

   _____ .

4. While it is not directly stated, the article suggests that
   a. Cortez was a god who came to the Aztecs as a plumed serpent.
   b. Cortez spread culture, civilization, and kindness in Mexico.
   c. Cortez destroyed a civilization without need or cause.

5. Something the Aztecs had never seen before were the Spaniards'
   a. horses.
   b. beards.
   c. feathers.

6. On the whole, the article tells about
   a. an accident of history that ended a civilization.
   b. the year on the Aztec calendar known as 1-Reed.
   c. the plumes that Hernando Cortez wore on his helmet.

7. Which statement does this article lead you to believe?
   a. Cortez is remembered in history as the man who saved the Aztec Empire.
   b. The Spaniards had no respect for the great Aztec culture.
   c. Conquerors usually have fair skins and beards and plumed helmets.

8. Why did Ce Malinalli help Cortez dress like a god?
   a. She thought she could become the companion of the conqueror.
   b. The messengers told her a secret about the gods.
   c. Montezuma had chosen her to welcome Cortez.

9. Think about the concept for this group of articles. Which statement seems true both for the article and for the concept?
   a. What will be, will be.
   b. What we don't know can hurt us.
   c. What we don't know can't hurt us.

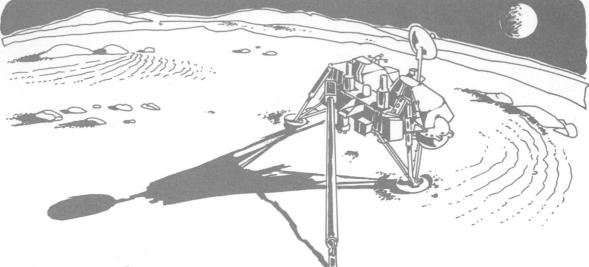

Probing the Planets

Mars and Venus are the planets nearest the earth. For many centuries, people have been eager to learn more about these close neighbors in our solar system. Since the Space Age began, scientists have built new tools to increase their knowledge of Mars and Venus. The most important of these tools are unmanned spacecraft called planetary probes.

American space scientists announced plans for the *Mariner* series of planetary probes in 1961. The launchings had to be made on certain days, determined by the positions of the earth, the sun, and Mars or Venus. Each probe would radio back to earth information collected by sensing instruments inside the spacecraft.

The first probe to return information about Venus was *Mariner 2*, launched on August 28, 1962. One hundred and nine days later it passed within 22,000 miles of Venus. *Mariner 5* was launched on June 14, 1967. It passed within 2,500 miles of Venus. On October 18, 1967, the Russian planetary probe *Venus 4*

planted an information-transmitting capsule on the surface of Venus.

Information radioed from the probes indicated that the surface temperatures on Venus may be as high as 800° F. The pressure of the atmosphere may be between 20 and 100 times that of the earth. The Venusian atmosphere is probably mostly carbon dioxide, with little water or oxygen.

The first probe to return information about Mars was *Mariner 4*, launched on November 28, 1964. Eight months later it passed within 6,200 miles of Mars and sent to earth twenty-one TV pictures of the surface.

In July 1976, Viking I arrived on the surface of Mars after an eleven-month journey. Almost at once, the unmanned craft started sending back to earth the first close-up pictures of Mars. They were in color and perfectly clear. They showed the dry, rocky surface of the red planet.

The craft was also equipped with special devices to take up soil samples. These would aid scientists at home in their search for life in the universe.

FIND THE ANSWERS

1. The planets nearest the earth are
   a. Saturn and Neptune.   c. Jupiter and Mars.
   b. Pluto and Uranus.   d. Mars and Venus.

2. The word in paragraph 1 that means *instruments used to explore or examine*

   is _____ .

3. The words "collected by sensing instruments inside the spacecraft" in para-

   graph 2 describe _____ .

4. While it is not directly stated, the article suggests that
   a. people keep adding to their information about the planets.
   b. the planets are too far away for people to learn anything.
   c. information about the planets is not very accurate.

5. The first probe to return information about Venus was
   a. *Mariner 2.*
   b. *Sputnik 8.*
   c. *Mars the 6.*

6. On the whole, the article tells about
   a. taking TV pictures of the surface of earth.
   b. studying the planets nearest the earth.
   c. the different names used for the many probes.

7. Which statement does this article lead you to believe?
   a. People probably cannot exist in the atmosphere of Venus.
   b. Most scientists think that humans are living on Venus now.
   c. Venus is farther from earth than Mars.

8. Why were launchings made only on certain days?
   a. Russians and Americans couldn't agree on the best days for launching.
   b. The scientists were superstitious about the right days for launchings.
   c. The earth, sun, and other planets had to be in the right positions.

9. Think about the concept for this group of articles. Which statement seems true
   both for the article and for the concept?
   a. People would rather have spacecraft come here from other planets.
   b. Scientists plan to probe other planets as soon as it is possible.
   c. Spacecraft that are sent to other planets must be unmanned.

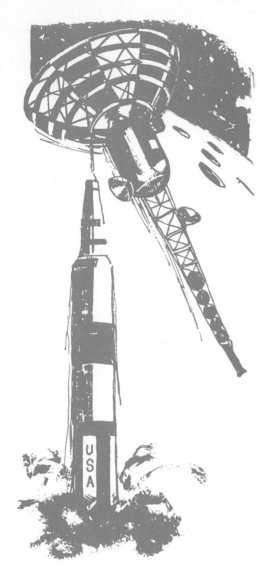

Explorer 1 *Saves the Day*

Explorer 1 was an artificial earth satellite designed and constructed in a hurry. It was launched by a rocket that was the second choice of scientists planning the first United States space effort. Yet *Explorer 1* made one of the greatest scientific discoveries of all time.

The project that was supposed to launch America's first artificial satellite into earth orbit was named Vanguard. On October 4, 1957, the Vanguard satellite was nearly ready for testing. But on that date, Russian scientists launched the world's first artificial satellite, *Sputnik 1*. The United States was surprised and disappointed to find itself behind in the space race. Work on the Vanguard project was speeded up. The launching was set for December 6. On that day, millions of television viewers saw the Vanguard rocket rise a few feet, then fall back and explode into flames.

An urgent call went out to Dr. Wernher von Braun, whose space research team was working on another rocket named Jupiter C. How soon could Jupiter C be ready to boost a new satellite into orbit?

About eight weeks later, on January 31, 1958, a Jupiter C rocket successfully placed in earth orbit the first United States artificial satellite, *Explorer 1*. Packed with scientific instruments, *Explorer 1* had been hastily constructed and weighed only 30 pounds. Yet *Explorer 1* sent back to earth more important information than had *Sputnik 2*, launched about the same time but thirty-six times heavier.

The most important information provided by *Explorer 1* indicated that a belt of intense radiation surrounded the earth. Dr. James A. Van Allen studied this information. He soon began mapping the radiation belt that now bears his name.

The fiery accident on the launch pad had made *Explorer 1*, rather than *Vanguard*, America's first satellite. Even more surprising, *Explorer 1* discovered the Van Allen radiation belt.

1. The world's first artificial satellite was named
   - a. *Sputnik 1.*   c. *Explorer 1.*
   - b. *Lika.*   d. *Vanguard.*

2. The word in paragraph 1 that means *made* or *built* is

   _____ .

3. The words "Packed with scientific instruments" in paragraph 4 describe the

   _____ .

4. While it is not directly stated, the article suggests that
   - a. Russia has brilliant scientists.
   - b. Americans are the best scientists.
   - c. there are scientists in only two countries.

5. America's first satellite was supposed to be the
   - a. *Uranus.*
   - b. *Vanguard.*
   - c. *Jupiter.*

6. On the whole, the article tells about
   - a. an American satellite which made an important discovery.
   - b. the launching of a satellite which failed to take off.
   - c. the different weights needed for all the satellites.

7. Which statement does this article lead you to believe?
   - a. Both Russia and the United States have given up space programs.
   - b. The Vanguard and Sputnik satellites were the only ones launched.
   - c. More artificial satellites have been launched since 1957.

8. Why was the United States surprised and disappointed when *Sputnik 1* was launched?
   - a. We were disappointed to hear there were scientists in Russia.
   - b. We were upset to find ourselves behind in the space race.
   - c. We were surprised at the name chosen for a space satellite.

9. Think about the concept for this group of articles. Which statement seems true both for the article and for the concept?
   - a. No one pays any attention to a discovery if it is not made on purpose.
   - b. Scientists do not approve of discoveries that are accidental.
   - c. Sometimes, unexpected accidents can change a scientific program.

A New Kind of Corn

In the 1920s the average yield of corn planted in the United States was 30 bushels to the acre. By the 1960s the average was 60 bushels to the acre. In some states the yield was even higher. Corn had changed. The stalks grew taller and stronger than those of the corn grown in the 1920s. The plants were better able to withstand drought and disease, and they bore more and larger ears. The new kind of corn was hybrid corn.

The experimenters who created hybrid corn carried out a great many tests in the years between 1900 and 1926. They controlled the fertilization of corn plants by tying paper bags over the tassels and over the growing ears. At just the right time, they transferred the pollen from the tassel to the silk on the ear. Then, they replaced the bag that covered the ear. No airborne pollen was allowed to touch the corn silk on a growing ear. In this way, each plant was fertilized with its own pollen, and inbred corn plants were the result. Several generations of inbreeding could fix good qualities in the corn plants, but the stalks tended to be weak and the ears small.

When pollen from one inbred plant was used to fertilize a different inbred plant, something exciting happened. The new seeds grew into plants that tended to have the qualities of both parents. But the new plants grew larger and stronger. This kind of crossbreeding is called hybridization, and the seed produced is hybrid seed.

After World War I, plant scientists worked out ways to make large amounts of hybrid seed available to farmers. Today, the new kind of corn, hybrid corn, adds millions of dollars to the income of America's farmers, and it helps to feed the world's growing population.

1. One kind of crossbreeding of plants is called
   - a. organization.
   - c. hybridization.
   - b. information.
   - d. colonization.

2. The word in paragraph 1 that means *the amount produced is*

   _____.

3. The words "taller and stronger than those of the corn grown in the 1920s" in

   paragraph 1 describe the _____.

4. While it is not directly stated, the article suggests that
   - a. the world needs more and more food all the time.
   - b. most people do not want to eat corn.
   - c. corn was good enough the way it was.

5. Experiments on corn were carried out in the years between
   - a. 1880 and 1900.
   - b. 1492 and 1776.
   - c. 1900 and 1926.

6. On the whole, the article tells about
   - a. the income of American farmers.
   - b. plants that looked like their parents.
   - c. the development of hybrid corn.

7. Which statement does this article lead you to believe?
   - a. Americans are the only people in the world who eat corn.
   - b. Farmers would rather not grow products from hybrid seed.
   - c. Fine corn takes a lot of care and skill to grow.

8. Why was hybrid corn better?
   - a. It had the best qualities of both parent corns.
   - b. It was grown in better fertilizer.
   - c. It had been stored for two generations.

9. Think about the concept for this group of articles. Which statement seems true
   both for the article and for the concept?
   - a. Inbred plants like corn are not safe to eat anymore.
   - b. Scientists should not interfere with natural things.
   - c. Hybrid corns are the result of careful planning by scientists.

The Plants That Escaped

Visitors to the New Orleans Cotton Exposition of 1884 saw a new tropical plant that had been brought from Venezuela. The new plant floated on the surface of a pond or stream. It was supported by an air-filled bladder in the stalk of each leaf. Each plant bore clusters of very beautiful orchidlike blossoms.

Some exposition visitors obtained cuttings of the plant to take home with them. They wanted the beautiful, pale-violet flowers floating on their garden pools. They got what they wanted and more, for the water hyacinth escaped from cultivation. It soon became a troublesome weed. Today, it chokes many streams and rivers in the southern United States, from Florida west to Texas.

Water hyacinths grow very quickly, covering the surface of a stream from bank to bank. One plant can produce 1,000 more plants in less than two months. The plants often form a tangled mass so thick that a boat can't force a way through it.

Because of their beauty, a few water hyacinths were imported into Africa. By the 1950s, the plant had clogged rivers that are important transportation routes in the Congo basin.

In the United States, a great deal of money has been spent on projects designed to control water hyacinths. Poisons will kill the plants and dredges can scoop them out of the water, but they soon reappear. Some scientists have suggested importing the sea cow into the southern United States. The sea cow is a large aquatic mammal that will eat water hyacinths.

Today, people are wiser about the accidents of nature than they were in 1884. Even so, no way has yet been found to control this beautiful plant that clogs so many waterways.

1. The new tropical plant was brought to New Orleans from
   - a. Venezuela.
   - b. Victoria.
   - c. Vancouver.
   - d. Virginia.

2. The word in paragraph 1 that means *bunches or groups of the same kind of thing growing together* is _____.

3. The words "a tangled mass so thick that a boat can't force a way through it" in paragraph 3 describe the _____.

4. While it is not directly stated, the article suggests that
   - a. nature can be too generous.
   - b. nature is always controlled.
   - c. there are no mistakes in nature.

5. A few water hyacinths were also imported into
   - a. Arctica.
   - b. Asia.
   - c. Africa.

6. On the whole, the article tells about
   - a. the difficulty in controlling a troublesome plant.
   - b. a Cotton Exposition held in New Orleans in 1884.
   - c. poisons and dredges used to kill certain plants.

7. Which statement does this article lead you to believe?
   - a. Hyacinths were planted to choke rivers from bank to bank.
   - b. Ships have no problem moving on rivers clogged with weeds.
   - c. In 1884 no one knew very much about the water hyacinths.

8. Why did some scientists suggest importing the sea cow?
   - a. The sea cow will eat water hyacinths.
   - b. Sea cows are scientists' favorite animals.
   - c. Sea cows look very attractive in the water.

9. Think about the concept for this group of articles. Which statement seems true both for the article and for the concept?
   - a. No scientific planning prepared for importing the water hyacinth.
   - b. Plans were made to clog the waterways with water hyacinths.
   - c. A weed cannot be troublesome if it has beautiful blossoms.

The Leakeys' Long Search

Dr. Louis S. B. Leakey was born in 1903 in East Africa. As a boy he roamed the wild bush country of Kenya with young African tribesmen. Sometimes he found odd-shaped stones. These he identified as the tools and weapons of prehistoric beings.

Louis Leakey was still a boy when he planned his life work. He decided to dig in Africa for more knowledge of prehistoric people and how they lived.

When he was older, Louis Leakey was sent to England to finish his education. When one teacher inquired about his plans for the future, he replied that he was going to study ancient humans in Africa. The teacher told him to go to Asia instead. No one expected important discoveries to be made in Africa.

But Leakey was the kind of person who believed in himself and in others. When Jane Goodall came to him with her plans to do research among African apes, Leakey helped her. Many people thought special training was necessary. But Dr. Leakey believed that if people had the interest and the will, special schooling wasn't needed.

Leakey continued his work, mostly at Olduvai (ōl'də wā') Gorge in Tanzania, a large nation just south of Kenya. He married a trained archeologist, Mary Nicol. Together, these great fossil hunters found thousands of crude stone tools at Olduvai Gorge. They unearthed the fossil bones of extinct animals that prehistoric humans had killed and eaten.

Finally, in the 1960s, Mary Leakey found the kind of fossil they had been hoping to find. It was a skull of a human-like creature who may be the oldest known ancestor of humans. Tests showed

that this being lived many millions of years ago. This discovery and others that followed helped convince scientists that Africa, rather than Asia, may have been humans' first home.

70

FIND THE ANSWERS

1. A large nation just south of Kenya is called
   - a. Turkey.
   - b. Tanzania.
   - c. Thailand.
   - d. Tasmania.

2. The word in paragraph 5 that means *went on with* is _____.

3. The words "the tools and weapons of prehistoric beings" in paragraph 1 describe the odd-shaped _____.

4. While it is not directly stated, the article suggests that
   - a. scientists once believed that the earliest humans lived in Asia.
   - b. scientists were once very much against archeologists.
   - c. scientists never take anybody's advice.

5. The Leakeys found thousands of crude stone tools at
   - a. Kenyan valleys.
   - b. East Asia
   - c. Olduvai Gorge.

6. On the whole, the article tells about
   - a. Dr. Louis Leakey's important teacher in England.
   - b. the Leakeys' search for the oldest known ancestors to humans.
   - c. the marriage of Dr. Leakey to a trained archeologist.

7. Which statement does this article lead you to believe?
   - a. Dr. Leakey convinced scientists that he could make crude tools.
   - b. Dr. Leakey should have gone to Asia as he was advised to do.
   - c. Dr. Leakey had the courage to follow his own convictions.

8. Why was Louis Leakey sent to England?
   - a. He was sent there to finish his education.
   - b. He was sent there to find prehistoric life.
   - c. He was sent there to learn about Africa.

9. Think about the concept for this group of articles. Which statement seems true both for the article and for the concept?
   - a. The Leakeys lived many millions of years ago.
   - b. The Leakeys' excavations followed a definite plan.
   - c. The Leakeys stumbled on prehistoric humans accidentally.

The Vanished Mandans

In the early 1800s, about 1,500 Mandan Indians lived in permanent villages along the upper Missouri River. In 1837 a steamboat came up the river, and white settlers visited the villages. Shortly thereafter, only thirty-one Mandans were left alive.

There had been no battle. It was not the enemies' guns that killed the Mandans, but an infectious disease against which the Indians had no resistance. Two of the outsiders who had visited the Mandan villages had been sick with smallpox.

The Mandans were the first of many Indian tribes to suffer from the great smallpox epidemic that swept the western plains between 1837 and 1841. The Mandans are of particular importance because they were among the most advanced of the Plains Indians. They hunted buffalo, but they also farmed, raising corn, beans, pumpkins, and sunflowers.

They built circular log houses forty to sixty feet in diameter, much larger and sturdier than most Indian dwellings.

Several Mandan families shared a house, but for privacy, each family had a curtained-off space near the outer walls. The Mandans had their own legends and ceremonials, and they made pottery and unusually handsome baskets.

This way of life disappeared with the Mandans in 1837.

The smallpox spread to the neighboring villages of the Arikari and Hidatsa Indians, where about half the 4,000 inhabitants died. Then the disease spread to the nomadic Plains Indians who lived farther west. It struck the Blackfeet, the Crow, the Sioux, the Pawnee, the Osage, the Kiowa, and the Comanche.

How many Indians died of smallpox? No one will ever know, as no records were kept. But many tribes lost half their people. By accident, the western Indians were half-defeated before United States soldiers set out to conquer them.

FIND THE ANSWERS

1. The Mandans were among the most advanced of the
    - a. River Indians.
    - b. Plains Indians.
    - c. Eastern Indians.
    - d. Desert Indians.

2. The word in paragraph 2 that means *spreading from one person to another* is
    _____ .

3. The words "forty to sixty feet in diameter" in paragraph 3 describe the
    _____   _____ .

4. While it is not directly stated, the article suggests that
    - a. it is not possible for one people to spread disease to others.
    - b. civilization does not always benefit a primitive people.
    - c. primitive people need to be exposed to many diseases.

5. Two visitors to the Mandan villages had been sick with
    - a. measles.
    - b. chickenpox.
    - c. smallpox.

6. On the whole, the article tells about
    - a. Indians who had ceremonials and legends.
    - b. the destruction of a people through disease.
    - c. the number of inhabitants in Mandan villages.

7. Which statement does this article lead you to believe?
    - a. Infectious diseases become epidemics only among Indian tribes.
    - b. The Mandan Indians refused to take medicine to help them get well.
    - c. There was no way to control infectious diseases in the 1800s.

8. Why did the Mandans' way of life disappear?
    - a. They were wiped out by stampeding buffalo.
    - b. The baskets they made did not sell.
    - c. Most of the people died of a smallpox epidemic.

9. Think about the concept for this group of articles. Which statement seems true both for the article and for the concept?
    - a. The settlers did not purposely infect the Indians with a disease.
    - b. The settlers were anxious to share their disease with the Indians.
    - c. The Indians should have planned to be away when the settlers came.

Taiwan on the Move

Taiwan is a small, mountainous island that lies about 700 miles southwest of Japan and just 100 miles off the coast of China. Taiwan is only 235 miles long and 90 miles wide. Three-fourths of its land is useless for farming. Yet Taiwan produces enough food for all its 13 million people and some for exporting. The island has to import raw materials for its factories, as it has few raw materials of its own. But in 1967 only one of the world's nations, Japan, had a faster rate of economic growth.

Taiwan is the home of the Chinese Nationalists who were forced to leave China in 1949. The political exiles settled on Taiwan.

Most of the 1½ million Chinese on Taiwan had little or no money, but they were willing to work hard. With American money and experts to help with planning, land reform and new industry brought wealth to Taiwan. Tenant farmers who had once paid out half their crops to absent landowners were helped to buy their own farms. Under new ownership, the farms produced more. Tax advantages were given to investors who started new factories to employ the intelligent and hard-working Taiwanese people.

Working together, the Taiwan Chinese and the Americans turned the crowded island into a prosperous new nation. In 1965, Taiwan announced that it needed no more economic help. By 1968, Taiwan was sending its own experts to other developing nations to help them plan ahead.

Today manufacturing contributes more to the island's economy than agriculture. Taiwan's busy factories turn out electronics components, refrigerators, umbrellas, toys, paper goods, motorcycles, fiberglass boats, and many other products. Some of these things are exported in ships built in Taiwan's own shipyards.

1. Taiwan today is supported mainly by its
   a. agriculture.
   b. manufacturing.
   c. rice products.
   d. American aid.

2. The word in the last paragraph that means *the necessary parts of something* is

   _____ .

3. The words "who had once paid out half their crops to absent landowners" in

   paragraph 3 describe the _____ _____ .

4. While it is not directly stated, the article suggests that
   a. Taiwan is too small to help itself.
   b. the Chinese are a lazy people.
   c. people want to help themselves.

5. Taiwan lies about 700 miles southwest of
   a. Japan.
   b. India.
   c. Suez.

6. On the whole, the article tells about
   a. factories on Taiwan that build ships.
   b. the economic progress of a tiny nation.
   c. Americans who made Taiwan too crowded.

7. Which statement does this article lead you to believe?
   a. The Chinese Nationalists are now leaving Taiwan.
   b. Taiwan is sending its experts to America to help us.
   c. Other nations are learning from Taiwan's example.

8. Why do you suppose Taiwan now depends more on industry than on farming?
   a. The people preferred factories to farming.
   b. The Taiwanese needed a great many refrigerators.
   c. Three-fourths of its land is useless for farming.

9. Think about the concept for this group of articles. Which statement seems true both for the article and for the concept?
   a. Agriculture is more important on Taiwan than manufacturing.
   b. No nation can ever support itself without help from America.
   c. With the proper planning, a nation can become self-supporting.

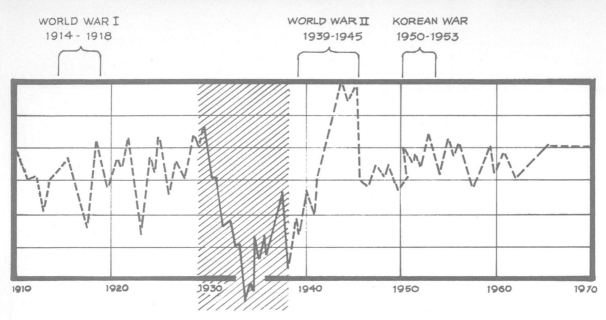

WORLD WAR I
1914 - 1918

WORLD WAR II
1939-1945

KOREAN WAR
1950-1953

1910   1920   1930   1940   1950   1960   1970

THE GREAT DEPRESSION BEGINNING 1929

Boom to Bust, 1929 to 1933

For most people in the United States, the 1920s were years of comfort, easy credit, and easy money. The stock market crash of October, 1929, was one event that changed the good times into hard times.

In the late 1920s, nearly everyone was certain that the easy credit and the good times would go on and on. Many were so confident that they borrowed from banks to buy cars, new homes, new furniture, clothing, and shares of stock in the ownership of America's big businesses. The stock market became a gambling place.

As long as stock prices went up, people could sell their stock shares at a profit and pay back what they had borrowed. But when stock prices fell, even a little, things changed. The banks demanded their money. To pay their debts, the borrowers had to sell their stocks for whatever they could get.

When a great many people have to sell stocks and few are eager to buy, stock prices plunge rapidly—and that is what happened in 1929.

Suddenly, people were less confident of the future. Many panicked and sold their stock shares. They stopped buying homes, cars, and furniture. Some factories had to close and many factory employees lost their jobs. Many stock shares became worthless. The Great Depression had begun.

People could not pay the banks the money they had borrowed, and the banks could not operate without money. Between 1930 and 1933, more than 9,000 banks closed. Many people lost their life savings.

Although the Great Depression affected the lives of millions of Americans, one after-effect was good. Laws were passed to insure wiser government control of stock transactions and banking procedures. Americans were determined not to undergo again the hard times of a severe depression.

1. The lives of millions of Americans were affected by the
    a. Gay Succession.   c. Grave Recession.
    b. Good Procession.   d. Great Depression.

2. The word in the last paragraph that means *ways of conducting a business* is

    _____ .

3. The words "a gambling place" in paragraph 2 describe the _____

    _____ .

4. While it is not directly stated, the article suggests that
    a. gambling on the stock market did no one any harm.
    b. people paid in advance for everything they bought.
    c. people were not managing their money carefully.

5. Banks could not operate without
    a. stocks.
    b. money.
    c. credit.

6. On the whole, the article tells about
    a. Americans who want to undergo a severe depression.
    b. people who passed laws to control the government.
    c. the cause and effect of a stock market crash.

7. Which statement does this article lead you to believe?
    a. The stock market crash ended hard times and brought good times.
    b. The stock market crash affected people who did not own stocks.
    c. The stock market crash only affected owners of certain stocks.

8. Why did borrowers have to sell their stocks?
    a. They wanted to see the stocks go down.
    b. They needed money to pay their debts.
    c. They hoped to get rich quick.

9. Think about the concept for this group of articles. Which statement seems true
    both for the article and for the concept?
    a. Stock prices that go up and down rapidly do not affect the economy.
    b. It is good for the economy when factory employees lose work.
    c. The need for controls in our economy was an unexpected lesson.

ITALY

PONTINE MARSHES

New Farms for Italy

Central Italy is mountainous and hilly, with some fertile valleys and some narrow plains. Near the coasts, the plains are often wet, low-lying areas with no slope, so that no drainage occurs. Water stands in shallow marshes. Mosquitoes breed and spread malaria.

Throughout history, the Italian people have gained much farmland by terracing their mountainsides and by draining their marshes with ditches and canals. But not until the 1930s did Italy reclaim the vast Pontine Marshes that covered about 300 square miles of land just south of Rome.

Through the centuries, malaria had made it almost impossible for men to live or work in the Pontine Marshes. A few people living on the mountainsides raised wheat in the marshes. But they stayed in the low unhealthy area only long enough to cultivate and harvest their crop. Grassy areas provided pasture

for a few cattle and sheep. Most of the Pontine Marshes remained unproductive and uninhabited.

In 160 B.C., the Romans made the first attempt to drain the Pontine Marshes — they failed. Another attempt was begun in the 1700s, but the work was not completed.

In 1931, the Italian government planned a new attack on the area's drainage problem. Using modern machinery, engineers dug ditches and canals through the Pontine Marshes. To force the marsh water toward the sea, pumping stations were built in the lowest places. Then, roads were built and modern towns were laid out. Homeless people were brought from the poorest parts of Italy to be settled on the reclaimed land.

Once the marshes were drained, malaria was conquered. Today, the huge swamp that was disease-ridden and nearly useless for so many centuries is rich farmland which helps feed Italy's people.

1. In the 1930s, Italy reclaimed the vast
   - a. mountainsides.
   - b. Plains Marches.
   - c. valley north of Rome.
   - d. Pontine Marshes.

2. The word in paragraph 1 that means *reproduce* is _____ .

3. The words "that was disease-ridden and nearly useless" in the last paragraph describe the huge _____ .

4. While it is not directly stated, the article suggests that
   - a. all farmland in Italy is found on mountains.
   - b. there is too much farmland in Central Italy.
   - c. farmland is important to the Italian people.

5. Pumping stations were built in the
   - a. lowest places.
   - b. highest places.
   - c. middle places.

6. On the whole, the article tells about
   - a. farmers who cultivate unhealthy crops.
   - b. reclaiming useless, disease-ridden land.
   - c. engineers who use only modern machinery.

7. Which statement does this article lead you to believe?
   - a. The Italian government should have allowed the area to stay useless.
   - b. Present-day Italians could not succeed where Romans failed.
   - c. People have wanted to make this land productive for centuries.

8. Why were homeless people brought from the poorest parts of Italy?
   - a. They were brought to conquer malaria on valley farms.
   - b. They were brought to spread their poverty over more area.
   - c. They were brought to help settle the reclaimed land.

9. Think about the concept for this group of articles. Which statement seems true both for the article and for the concept?
   - a. Modern engineering helps good planning succeed.
   - b. It is useless to plan new ways to farm.
   - c. All Italian farmland was once completely useless.

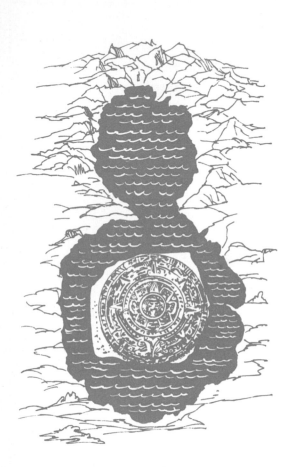

Mexico's Lost Lakes

The heart of Mexico is a high, oval valley surrounded by mountains. Once, forests blanketed the mountainsides, and broad, shining lakes covered nearly all the valley floor. Now, the mountains are bare and scarred with erosion, and much of the valley floor is dry and dusty.

Cortez and his Spanish soldiers were the first Europeans to enter this valley. They saw the flourishing Aztec city of Tenochtitlan (tā näch'tē tlän') rising from an island in one of the lakes. Surrounding it were green floating gardens. The Spaniards said it was as beautiful as a dream. Then the conquest began.

By 1521, when the Spaniards had conquered the fierce Aztecs, the island city was in ruins. Cortez decided to rebuild it after the pattern of European cities. Using the conquered Aztecs as slave laborers, Cortez built the new city, now Mexico City, in just four years.

"But a generation had scarcely passed after the Conquest before a sad change came over these scenes so beautiful," writes one historian. The broad, shining lakes began to dry up.

Modern historians believe that Cortez began the destruction of the valley's lakes when he ordered the city rebuilt. A great deal of charcoal was needed to burn the limestone from which cement and mortar were made. Wood was needed to finish the interiors of the buildings.

The mountainside forests were destroyed to provide the charcoal and wood. Once the slopes were bare, rainfall no longer seeped slowly into the earth to feed the springs that filled the valley's lakes. Instead, rainfall poured off the mountainsides and caused periodic flooding of the valley. To protect the city from floods, later rulers made a cut through the mountains so that the water drained away into another valley. Mexico City, once an island, had become a city on a dry plain.

1. Mexico City was once an
   a. atoll.
   b. archipelago.
   c. island.
   d. eyesore.

2. The word in paragraph 5 that means *a material used to hold stones or bricks together* is _____ .

3. The words "to feed the springs that filled the valley's lakes" in the last paragraph describe the _____ .

4. While it is not directly stated, the article suggests that
   a. the Aztecs didn't begin to flourish until Cortez came.
   b. the Spaniards destroyed a civilization as well as a city.
   c. the Spaniards brought a fine civilization to the Aztecs.

5. Mountainside forests were destroyed to provide
   a. charcoal and wood.
   b. rainfall and clay.
   c. chariots and wool.

6. On the whole, the article tells about
   a. Mexico City before and after the Spaniards came.
   b. Mexico as it looked when it was a European city.
   c. modern historians who write about Mexico City.

7. Which statement does this article lead you to believe?
   a. Keeping nature's balance is not important anymore.
   b. People thought nature's resources would last forever.
   c. New forests always automatically replace old ones.

8. Why did later rulers cut through the mountains?
   a. They wanted to fill the city with rainwater.
   b. They wanted to protect the city from floods.
   c. They wanted the valleys to flood regularly.

9. Think about the concept for this group of articles. Which statement seems true both for the article and for the concept?
   a. Rainfall is needed only in mountain areas now.
   b. Too many lakes spoil the appearance of the land.
   c. Cortez believed he was building a better city.

Fighting Fog

To airlines and airport operators, fog is an enemy. When the white, misty blanket hides runways, airplanes cannot take off or land. Changes in flight schedules cost the airlines several million dollars each year.

Fog is a concentration of tiny water droplets suspended in the air. It most often occurs when warm, moist air is suddenly cooled. To clear the air of fog, it is necessary to evaporate the droplets or cause them to join together and fall as rain or snow.

In 1968, a new fog-sweeping machine was tested for dissipating the most common kind of fog, which occurs at temperatures above freezing. The machine consisted of a 100-foot-long plastic tube mounted on a mobile blower. As the machine moved across the airport, chemicals were blown through the tube and up into the fog. One of the chemicals reduced the surface tension on the water droplets so that they would join together more easily. Another chemical gave an electrical charge to the droplets, so that they attracted each other and fell as rain.

Cold fog, which occurs at temperatures below freezing, causes only a small percentage of airport shutdowns. Cold fog is fairly easy to eliminate. For quite a few years, airports have used cloud-seeding methods to dissipate cold fog. An airplane drops crystals of dry ice into the fog. Soon, snow falls and the air clears.

In 1969, the United States Air Force announced a plan for use when warm, dry air lies over a layer of cold fog. A helicopter hovers over the fog layer. The whirling rotor blades push warm, dry air down to mix with the foggy layer and cause the water droplets to evaporate.

Someday, these new "weather weapons" may win our war against fog.

FIND THE ANSWERS

1. One chemical gave the droplets
   a. an electrical charge.   c. a mobile blower.
   b. extra surface tension.   d. an old fog layer.

2. The word in paragraph 3 that means *separating* or *scattering in several directions* is _____ .

3. The words "a 100-foot-long plastic tube mounted on a mobile blower" in paragraph 3 describe the _____ .

4. While it is not directly stated, the article suggests that
   a. fog can be dangerous.
   b. fog is not important.
   c. fog can always be cleared.

5. To dissipate fog, some airports have used
   a. tiny water droplets.
   b. cloud-seeding methods.
   c. snow and ice cubes.

6. On the whole, the article tells about
   a. the temperature needed to make a cold fog appear.
   b. the "weather weapons" people use when they go to war.
   c. different methods used to clear fog at airports.

7. Which statement does this article lead you to believe?
   a. Some methods of clearing fog have already been successful.
   b. There is a law against using helicopters to help clear fog.
   c. The only successful way to clear fog is by cloud-seeding.

8. Why can't airplanes land or take off when it is foggy?
   a. Fog forms crystals of dry ice on the airplanes.
   b. They have to wait for helicopters in fog layers.
   c. The white, misty blanket hides the runways.

9. Think about the concept for this group of articles. Which statement seems true both for the article and for the concept?
   a. Someday people plan to be able to control fog completely.
   b. People should not hope to control fog completely.
   c. There are too many "weather weapons" being used.

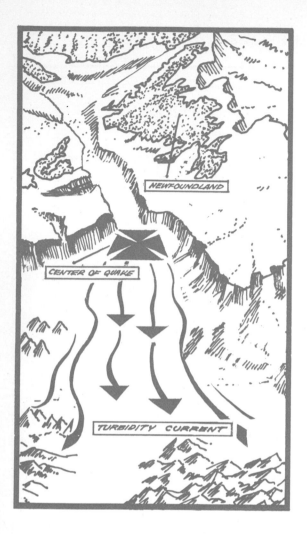

NEWFOUNDLAND

CENTER OF QUAKE

TURBIDITY CURRENT

off to the bottom of the sea. The quake occurred in an area crossed by many transatlantic telegraph cables lying on the ocean floor.

At the time of the quake, six of the nearest cables stopped transmitting messages. These cables were broken by the earthquake. Hours later, three other cables, which lay further south, stopped transmitting messages. No one knew what broke them. Cables a similar distance to the north were not affected.

Like detectives trying to solve a mysterious crime, scientists studied the clues. Eventually, they became convinced that the earthquake had created a turbidity current that had flowed more than 600 miles down the continental slope to break the three southernmost cables.

The earthquake had stirred up mud on the continental slope, creating a huge mass of muddy water much heavier than the water around it. Responding to gravity, the muddy water had flowed down the steep slope. As it moved, the turbidity current picked up speed and sediment. Because the scientists knew at what times the different cables had stopped transmitting, they were able to estimate how fast the current had flowed. The current had broken the last cable thirteen hours after the earthquake.

Today, scientists believe that turbidity currents help create the steep-sided submarine canyons that cut into the continental slope. Just as a river deepens a valley on land, a turbidity current can scour out a canyon under the sea.

The 1929 earthquake interrupted transatlantic telegraph service. But it added much to our knowledge of the mysterious forces of the sea.

An Undersea Mystery

Turbidity currents are like angry, muddy rivers that flow under the surface of the sea. Until recently, scientists were not sure such currents existed. In 1929, an underwater earthquake south of Newfoundland helped scientists learn about turbidity currents.

The earthquake was centered below the continental slope. This slope marks the edge of the more gently-sloping continental shelf. It is the steep drop-

1. In 1929, an underwater earthquake took place
   a. north of Nova Scotia.
   b. south of Newfoundland.
   c. west of New Mexico.
   d. east of Norway.

2. The word in paragraph 4 that means *secret, unknown, or unexplainable* is

   _____ .

3. The words "angry, muddy rivers that flow under the surface of the sea" in

   paragraph 1 describe _____ _____ .

4. While it is not directly stated, the article suggests that
   a. scientists can keep track of underwater earthquakes.
   b. it is impossible to tell when earthquakes take place.
   c. earthquakes cause damage only when they are on the surface.

5. A turbidity current can scour out a canyon
   a. through a hill.
   b. in a mountain.
   c. under the sea.

6. On the whole, the article tells about
   a. the outer limit of the gently-sloping continental shelf.
   b. muddy waters that break cables every thirteen hours.
   c. an earthquake that added to our knowledge of the sea.

7. Which statement does this article lead you to believe?
   a. We have no idea what the ocean floor is like.
   b. The ocean floor may have many features like those on the continents.
   c. The entire ocean floor is smooth and flat.

8. Why did the muddy water flow down the slope?
   a. It was responding to gravity.
   b. It had no place else to go.
   c. It was trying to get to the cables.

9. Think about the concept for this group of articles. Which statement seems true both for the article and for the concept?
   a. The only harm earthquakes can cause is broken cables.
   b. Violence in nature can sometimes have helpful side-effects.
   c. Nothing good can ever come from turbidity currents.

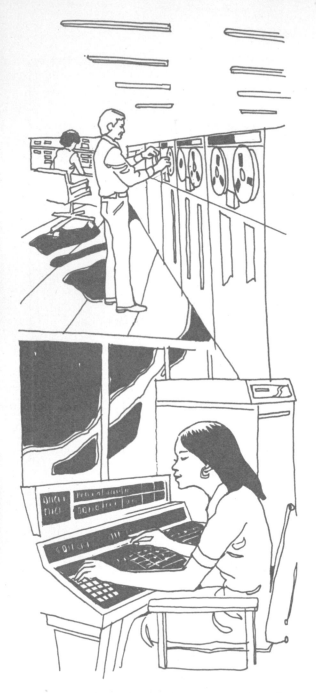

The first modern computers were built in the 1930s. They were not electric, as are today's computers. These first modern computers were mechanical monsters that filled huge rooms. A few years later, the bulky gears and shafts were replaced with electrical switches, telephone relays, and vacuum tubes. In the 1950s, transistors replaced the vacuum tubes. Transistors do the same work as vacuum tubes but are much smaller and lighter.

In the 1960s, even smaller electronic parts called monolithic block crystals came into use. The monolithic block crystals replaced the transistors and much of the wiring in computers. Some of these newest computers are small enough to be held in your hand. Such computers are often used in spacecraft, where small size and light weight are so important.

The same developments that reduced the computer's size and weight also increased its speed. Computers built in the 1930s could perform a calculation in addition in one-third of a second. The first electronic computer, built in 1946, could add in one five-thousandth of a second. The newest generation of computers can add faster than one ten-millionth of a second.

The rapid increase in computer speed has made possible the solving of problems far beyond the reach of early computers. The newest computers work about 10 million times as fast as the first modern computers. Even so, on the fastest of today's computers, multiplication takes about three times as long as addition. Mathematicians believe that someday, computers will be able to do one kind of calculation just as fast as another.

Fast — But Not Fast Enough

Computers are not only changing the world we live in — computers themselves are changing. They are becoming lighter, faster, and smaller.

FIND THE ANSWERS

1. The monolithic block crystals replaced the
   - a. computers.
   - b. electronics.
   - c. transistors.
   - d. transgressors.

2. The word in paragraph 4 that means *the act of counting or estimating* is

   _____.

3. The words "small enough to be held in your hand" in paragraph 3 describe

   some of the newest _____.

4. While it is not directly stated, the article suggests that
   - a. small-size, lightweight computers are not allowed on spacecraft.
   - b. the computers we have now are perfect and do not need to be better.
   - c. computers of the future will be superior to those we have now.

5. Smaller electronic parts came into use in the
   - a. 1680s.
   - b. 1960s.
   - c. 1890s.

6. On the whole, the article tells about
   - a. mathematicians and what they believe.
   - b. the first electronic computer ever built.
   - c. important developments in modern computers.

7. Which statement does this article lead you to believe?
   - a. The increase in speed has made new problems for computers.
   - b. Computers take too long to do their calculations.
   - c. A computer can calculate faster than a person can.

8. Why did monolithic block crystals improve computers?

   - a. They replaced transistors and much wiring.
   - b. They were mechanical and introduced transistors.
   - c. They made possible electrical switches.

9. Think about the concept for this group of articles. Which statement seems true
   both for the article and for the concept?
   - a. Vacuum tubes have replaced electricity and telephones.
   - b. People will continue to try to improve our computers.
   - c. Plans that reduced the speed of computers failed.

Revolution in the Classroom

In 1957, Russian space scientists launched the first artificial satellite, *Sputnik*, into earth orbit. Americans were shocked and surprised. Until *Sputnik*, most Americans believed that their country was well ahead of other countries in scientific knowledge.

After *Sputnik*, many Americans took a long, hard look at their own school system. They wanted to be sure that American schools were properly preparing young people to join in the race for new knowledge. In particular, they wanted to make sure young people were being prepared for careers in science.

Mathematicians were quick to point out that in their field American schools were far behind the times. The schools taught only math known before the 1700s. They depended on out-of-date teaching methods. Boys and girls memorized rules and then used the rules to solve math problems. Few students understood the "whys" behind the rules. Most students found mathematics dull and tiresome. Few went on to study advanced mathematics in high school. Therefore, few were being prepared to study science, which depends so much on mathematics.

A few school systems had been experimenting with new methods of teaching mathematics. After *Sputnik*, the government provided money for expanding such programs. Soon, expert teachers were busy planning new courses of study and writing new textbooks.

From this planning came the "new math," which stresses the understanding of concepts rather than the memorizing of rules. "New math" attempts to show how all of mathematics is a logical system containing relationships and patterns that students can discover for themselves.

The new methods of teaching mathematics replaced the old ones in many of America's schools. Sputnik began a revolution in the classroom. Today new revolutions in teaching are changing our classrooms again. Can you think of changes going on in your school?

FIND THE ANSWERS

1. The first artificial satellite was launched by
   a. Spain.
   b. Russia.
   c. England.
   d. America.

2. The word in paragraph 5 that means *emphasizes the importance of* is

   _____ .

3. The words "dull and tiresome" in paragraph 3 describe the old

   _____ .

4. While it is not directly stated, the article suggests that
   a. methods of teaching should change from time to time.
   b. subjects should always be taught in the same way.
   c. most students found mathematics an exciting subject.

5. Mathematics is important for a career in
   a. philosophy.
   b. racing.
   c. science.

6. On the whole, the article tells about
   a. the date *Sputnik* went into orbit.
   b. the introduction of "new math."
   c. mathematicians in the United States.

7. Which statement does this article lead you to believe?
   a. Children understood math better before the 1700s.
   b. Two-thirds of America's schools do not teach math.
   c. Scientific advances can cause world-wide changes.

8. Why were Americans shocked and surprised when *Sputnik* went into orbit?
   a. They believed it was against the law to orbit a satellite.
   b. They thought America led the world in scientific knowledge.
   c. They didn't think a Russian satellite belonged in space.

9. Think about the concept for this group of articles. Which statement seems true both for the article and for the concept?
   a. All young people in Russia study to be space scientists.
   b. Russian scientists want Americans to study the "new math."
   c. Math in American schools was changed unexpectedly by Russian scientists.

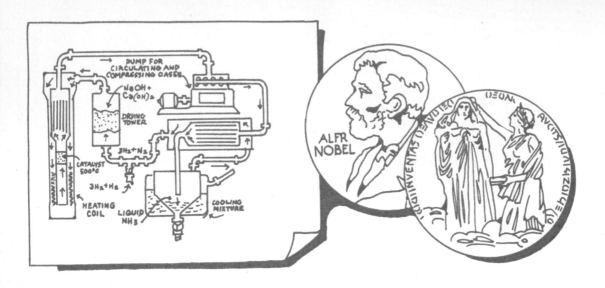

A Chemist Finds a Way

Except for coal, Germany has never had the great supplies of raw materials that an industrial nation needs. Yet Germany has many industries. Some of them were made possible by its scientists. These scientists found ways to produce raw materials Germany needed from the few raw materials that Germany had.

Until the beginning of World War I, Germany imported large amounts of nitrogen compounds from Chile. Some nitrogen compounds occur naturally in the soil. Germany used these imported nitrogen compounds to produce chemicals such as ammonia, a necessary ingredient in explosives and fertilizers.

When World War I began in 1914, British ships moved quickly to blockade Germany's seaports. Because of the blockade, Germany could no longer import nitrogen compounds from South America, just at a time when they were needed more than ever before. To carry on the war, the German army had to have ammonia to make its explosives. To produce enough food for the people to eat, German farmers had to have fertilizers.

In 1914, the German chemist Fritz Haber offered his services to his government. He knew how important nitrogen compounds were to the war effort. Fritz Haber had already planned and developed new ways to produce them. From his thinking came a new process for producing ammonia by mixing nitrogen from air with hydrogen from water. A fellow scientist, Carl Bosch, adapted the process for industrial use. The synthetic ammonia was used to make the explosives and fertilizers that Germany needed to carry on the war.

Although the Haber-Bosch process was a response to a wartime need, it has proved widely useful in peacetime. For his work, Fritz Haber received the 1918 Nobel Prize in chemistry. The world's great industries owe much to the scientists who plan ways to make materials people need from the raw materials at hand.

FIND THE ANSWERS

1. One of Germany's few raw materials has been
   - a. bronze.   c. iron.
   - b. copper.   d. coal.

2. The word in paragraph 4 that means changed or made to fit some thing else

   is _____.

3. The words "who plan ways to make materials people need" in the last para-

   graph describe _____.

4. While it is not directly stated, the article suggests that
   - a. all of Germany's scientists refused to help their country.
   - b. most governments find their scientists cannot help them.
   - c. scientists are of great importance to their governments.

5. To carry on the war, the German army had to have
   - a. ammonia.
   - b. azaleas.
   - c. Arizona.

6. On the whole, the article tells about
   - a. German farmers who wanted fertilizers.
   - b. the creation of new products in wartime.
   - c. the 1918 Nobel Prize given to artists.

7. Which statement does this article lead you to believe?
   - a. A scientific process can apply to many fields.
   - b. All scientists must now be chemists only.
   - c. South American scientists have gone to Germany.

8. Why wouldn't Germany import nitrogen compounds?
   - a. It preferred to import hydrogen instead.
   - b. Its ports were blockaded by England.
   - c. South America ran out of the compounds.

9. Think about the concept for this group of articles. Which statement seems true
   both for the article and for the concept?
   - a. A war emergency is the only thing that creates new ideas.
   - b. Anything planned during an emergency will always fail.
   - c. Good plans sometimes are the result of emergencies.

A Lucky Accident

In the early 1800s, people were fascinated by the curious substance made from the sap of tropical American trees. The substance was pure rubber. From it, balls were made for children's play, and erasers for rubbing out pencil marks. Pure rubber was used to make boots and waterproof cloth for raincoats, but these articles often hardened or melted in the changeable climate of North America.

Pure rubber melts when it is heated, and turns hard and brittle when it is chilled. Before rubber could be used for most purposes, it had to be changed in a way that would make it tougher and more resistant to extremes of temperature.

A young hardware merchant from Connecticut was one of the persons interested in the stretchy, bouncy substance. His name was Charles Goodyear. Convinced that pure rubber had great possibilities, he neglected his business to experiment with it. His business failed, and he was jailed for debt. Once he even sold his children's schoolbooks to get money to carry on his experiments.

Yet Goodyear succeeded where others experimenting with rubber failed. He tried mixing pure rubber with sulfur.

Accidently, he dropped some of this mixture on a hot stove. To his surprise, this rubber did not melt when hot. When it was cooled, it was still stretchy. He nailed it to the outside of a doorframe and left it overnight, but the frost did not make it hard and brittle.

Goodyear named his process of heating rubber and sulfur "vulcanization," after Vulcan, the Roman god of fire. Vulcanized rubber made possible bicycle tires, pulley belts, and rubber parts for machinery. Later, automobile tires and a thousand other useful articles were manufactured from Charles Goodyear's "accident": vulcanized rubber.

1. Goodyear tried mixing pure rubber with
    a. plasma.   c. crystals.
    b. topsoil.   d. sulfur.

2. The word in paragraph 2 that means *easily broken* is _____.

3. The words "from the sap of tropical American trees" in paragraph 1 describe
    the curious _____.

4. While it is not directly stated, the article suggests that
    a. vulcanized rubber is used in many industries.
    b. useful articles cannot be made from rubber.
    c. vulcanized rubber comes from American trees.

5. "Vulcanization" was named for Vulcan,
    a. the Trojan god of war.
    b. the Roman god of fire.
    c. the Greek god of sulfur.

6. On the whole, the article tells about
    a. products made from pure rubber.
    b. the changeable climate of North America.
    c. Goodyear's discovery of vulcanized rubber.

7. Which statement does this article lead you to believe?
    a. Vulcanized rubber is the only product discovered by accident.
    b. When experiments fail, inventors should stop experimenting.
    c. Many new products were created with the use of vulcanized rubber.

8. What is one reason vulcanized rubber is better than pure rubber?
    a. Vulcanized rubber is not affected by climate.
    b. Boots and erasers cannot be made from pure rubber.
    c. Vulcanized rubber is made from pure sulfur.

9. Think about the concept for this group of articles. Which statement seems true
    both for the article and for the concept?
    a. An important discovery can be made by accident.
    b. Goodyear succeeded because his business failed.
    c. An invention can never come about by chance.

The Eskimo Artists

Carving was once the Eskimos' way of making the tools and utensils they needed to live. From ivory, bone, and driftwood, they carved knife handles, harpoons, and buttons. From soapstone they carved oil lamps and cooking pots.

Today, Eskimos buy factory-made tools and utensils instead of carving them. But Eskimos continue to carve as a means of artistic expression and as a way to earn money. Eskimo carvings are shown in museums and art galleries, and they are sold in many city gift shops.

The popularity of Eskimo carving was sparked by James Houston, an artist who made a painting trip to Northern Canada in 1948. Visiting Port Harrison on Hudson Bay, he learned how a dwindling supply of game made it difficult for the Eskimos to earn a living by fur trapping.

Houston admired some small soapstone statues carved by the Port Harrison Eskimos. He recognized their natural talent as artists. They needed only encouragement and help in marketing their work.

Much of the Eskimo art Houston saw portrays Arctic birds and animals and parka-clad Eskimos working at traditional tasks. The best pieces express the Eskimo's pride in the old way of life, the way of the hunter.

In Montreal and other Canadian cities, Houston showed samples of Eskimo carving. He also discussed his plan for helping the Eskimos. Backed by private citizens and later by the Canadian government, he made many trips to settlements in the far north. There, he urged more Eskimos to take up carving and other art forms. Houston bought the

pieces and shipped them south to be sold.

Thanks to the encouragement and help of James Houston, Eskimo art is now sold and admired all over the world. And through their art, many Eskimos are earning a better living than before.

94

FIND THE ANSWERS

1. Houston admired some small soapstone statues carved by the
   - a. Port Harrison Eskimos.
   - b. Fort Morrison Indians.
   - c. Montreal Eskimos.
   - d. Antarctic Indians.

2. The word in paragraph 5 that means *pictures* or *represents as in a drawing* is

   _____ .

3. The words "an artist who made a painting trip to Northern Canada" in para-

   graph 3 describe _____ _____ .

4. While it is not directly stated, the article suggests that
   - a. primitive people use materials at hand in their art.
   - b. primitive people are not interested in art forms.
   - c. carvings and statues are not good art expressions.

5. Houston showed samples of the carving in
   - a. Madison.
   - b. Montreal.
   - c. Montauk.

6. On the whole, the article tells about
   - a. one artist's efforts to encourage Eskimo art.
   - b. factory-made tools and utensils sold to Eskimos.
   - c. painting trips made to Northern Canada by Houston.

7. Which statement does this article lead you to believe?
   - a. People around the world like Eskimo art.
   - b. Eskimo art is sold only in parts of Canada now.
   - c. The best pieces of Eskimo art portray Houston.

8. Why was it difficult for Eskimos to earn a living by fur trapping?
   - a. Fur trapping is too hard for Eskimos.
   - b. The Eskimos were too lazy to hunt.
   - c. The supply of game was dwindling.

9. Think about the concept for this group of articles. Which statement seems true both for the article and for the concept?
   - a. Earning money through art was planned by an interested outsider.
   - b. Eskimos do not need to earn money because they have great talent.
   - c. Eskimos continue to earn money by making utensils for factories.

A New Craft for the Navahos

The Navaho Indians of Arizona and New Mexico are well known for their work with silver. They make silver bracelets and belt buckles stamped with intricate patterns of wavy lines, crescent moons, and arrowheads. They make silver rings set with turquoise stones.

Many people proudly wear Navaho jewelry. Navaho silverwork is often shown in museums and art galleries.

Most people are surprised to learn that silversmithing is not an ancient art of the Navahos. It is likely that they did not learn much about working with silver until about 1869. Before that time, the Navahos obtained most of their silver jewelry from Mexican villages south of the border.

The Mexicans were skilled silversmiths, but the Navahos did not have much chance to learn the craft from them because the two peoples were enemies. The Navahos repeatedly raided Mexican villages.

This border warfare between Navahos and Mexicans made trouble for the United States government. Finally Colonel Kit Carson was sent with United States Army troops to enforce a peace. When other measures failed, the Navahos were confined at Fort Sumner for about four years.

During 1867 and 1868, the Navahos were freed. They returned to their old territory, where they were given new livestock by the United States government. There were no more raids across the border. Instead, Navahos peacefully watched Mexican silversmiths at work and learned from them. Soon the Navahos were melting down silver coins and reshaping the metal into ornaments. They began to earn money by selling silver jewelry to other Indians, and to tourists who visited the Navaho reservation.

The peace that followed the border warfare brought the Navahos an unexpected benefit. It gave them a chance to learn a new and profitable craft— a craft at which they became experts.

1. The Mexicans were skilled
   a. silversmiths.
   b. locksmiths.
   c. blacksmiths.
   d. goldsmiths.

2. The word in paragraph 1 that means *complicated* is _____.

3. The words "who visited the Navaho reservation" in paragraph 5 describe the

   _____.

4. While it is not directly stated, the article suggests that
   a. neighbors always war with each other.
   b. the effort that goes into warfare can be put to better use.
   c. warfare often results in people learning from one another.

5. During 1867 and 1868, the Navahos were
   a. found.
   b. chained.
   c. freed.

6. On the whole, the article tells about
   a. the livestock given to all the Navahos.
   b. Mexicans who visited Navaho reservations.
   c. a craft one people learned from another.

7. Which statement does the article lead you to believe?
   a. Tourists are glad to buy Navaho jewelry.
   b. Navaho jewelry is made mostly by tourists.
   c. Tourists cannot buy any Navaho jewelry.

8. Why did the United States government send troops?
   a. The troops heard the Mexicans had silver.
   b. The troops wanted to recruit the Navahos.
   c. The troops were sent to enforce a peace.

9. Think about the concept for this group of articles. Which statement seems true both for the article and for the concept?
   a. Art must be planned to be successful.
   b. New art forms grow in unexpected ways.
   c. Only modern people accept new art forms.

The Sun Sisters

Who lives in the sun? A fire dragon? A god of fire? Some say that it is really a golden raven. And that is why the Chinese make a special sign for the sun —a bird in a circle. But why can't you look into the sun? You can look at the moon and see shapes and faces, but the sun is different.

The Chinese tell a tale about the sun. It goes like this.

Long, long ago, a young man lived in the sun. He had two young sisters who lived in the moon. It is said of these two sisters that they were quite beautiful. People said that they were like two blossoms in a garden.

People told of their beauty, which was like the beauty of nature. The sisters were slender as the bamboo. They were as graceful as willow branches. Their faces were shaped like the oval seeds of the melon. Their hair was like the black of night, and around their dark eyes were circles as white as the snow.

The beauty of the sisters was known throughout the land. But they were not only beautiful. They were as clever as they were beautiful. They spent their days stitching with embroidery needles.

They were very skilled. They covered their silken robes with the finest stitches. They covered their delicate slippers with stitches just as delicate. They could make flowers lovelier than any in the garden.

They stitched dragons, birds, and butterflies with thousands of fine, tiny stitches. Their robes looked like the paintings of the greatest painters.

All night, the sisters stitched by the light of the moon. The skill of these sisters spread throughout the land. People heard of the beauty of their robes made with the finest of stitches. On clear nights, people gathered in their gardens. They strained their eyes to see these wonderful sisters in the moon. They climbed the hills and mountains to look up at the moon. They wanted to catch a glimpse of these young women.

From their high palace, the sisters watched. And they were not at all pleased. At that time, it was the custom that young maidens were not to be stared at, especially by young men.

As the sisters watched the people below, they became distressed. So many people came out at night to gaze at them. What could they do? Each night as they stitched, they began to think of ways to avoid the stares. With each tiny stitch, they searched their minds. They thought of hiding, but they disliked that idea. They had done nothing wrong, why should they hide?

Finally, one of the sisters said, "I think I have the solution. We will go to our dear brother in the sun and ask him to change places with us. We will live in the sun and he will live in the moon."

"What a wonderful plan!" said her sister. "We must leave at once to visit our brother in the sun." The two sisters put on their finest robes and set off to present their plan.

As they approached the shining palace in the sun, they called out to their brother. "Oh, great and wise brother, we have had great problems."

"What can be troubling you, my sisters? You are fair and talented and you have each other for company. What can possibly be troubling you?"

One of the sisters spoke up. "It is true, my brother, we are quite lucky to have such beauty around us. We love to be with one another and we love each minute that we stitch our colorful designs. But the trouble is not with us. It is with others."

"Yes," said the other sister, afraid that they had displeased their brother. "We are happy in our home, but we are not happy with the people below. Each night, when people come out in their gardens, they stare up at us. It should not be like this. We are unhappy."

Their brother was not happy when he heard their story. He agreed that it was not proper for the people to stare. "Well, I will think of a plan," the brother offered.

"If it please you, my brother, we have spent long hours thinking of a plan of our own. We think it will work." Then the sisters told him of their plan to live in the sun.

The brother listened carefully. He began to laugh. "Now, you are really being silly," he told them. "If you are

bothered by people at night, what will happen by day? In the daylight, when my sunlight shines, there are many, many more people awake than at night. If you change places with me, what will you do with these thousands more eyes that will be gazing at you?"

The sisters did not mind their brother's protests. They insisted, "Oh, please, dear brother, if you will just cooperate with us, you will learn that we have a way to make our plan work. You must trust us and we will be successful."

The brother had great doubts, but he loved his sisters, and he knew that they were not foolish. At last, he agreed and made plans to change places with his sisters. He would dwell in the moon and they would take his place in the sun.

The sisters were delighted. They sang as they gathered their beautiful robes and their delicate slippers. These precious belongings were carefully packed into a shiny red chest. They placed their tiny needles in a special case. This, too, was placed most carefully into the shiny red chest.

With their precious robes packed and their precious needles safe, they quickly made their way to their new home. In no time at all, they were completely settled in their bright dwelling.

At night, the people below came out to look for the sisters. They were bewildered. What had happened to the beauties in the moon? Quickly, the word spread. If they wished to see the beauty of the sisters, they must look to the sun.

Thousands of curious eyes gazed into the daytime skies. But the sisters plan protected them. People turned away in pain. Each time the people would gaze up at them, the sisters would sting them with their tiny, sharp embroidery needles. "The sun's rays are too bright," people said. "They hurt our eyes." Try as they might, the people below could never again glimpse the two sisters.

Perhaps you, too, have tried to gaze at the sun and have felt your eyes sting as a result. Perhaps the sisters' plan is still working.   (1105 words)

III

Modern Ways of Life
Require Planned Change

In this section you will read about many ways in which people must plan for the future. You will read about these things in the areas of history, space, biology, anthropology, economics, geography, earth science, mathematics, engineering, and art.

Keep these questions in mind when you are reading.

1. What are some planned changes that have affected our country?

2. What are some planned changes that have affected us as individuals?

3. Are all planned changes necessarily good?

4. If all changes are not good, what can you do to correct the change?

5. What planning must take place to cause changes to occur?

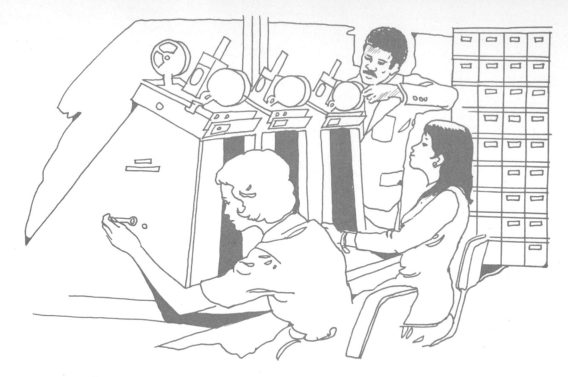

History on Film

Not long ago, most historians had to be travelers. To consult written accounts of historical events, they had to travel to the places where the accounts were stored. To read rare old books and other documents, they often had to visit museums and libraries far from home.

Today, historians can examine many old books and documents without traveling very far. Rare books, old letters, and other historical documents are being microfilmed. Many different libraries can now have copies.

Microfilming is a photographic process which copies and reduces pages of printed or written matter to small reels of film. To read microfilm, the user places the reel in a machine. The machine then projects a full-sized image on a glass screen. Up to 5,000 book pages can be copied on one reel of microfilm. A reel takes up less storage space than a book and can be mailed with ease.

Once a rare book or other document has been microfilmed, the original can be stored and protected from damage or theft. Some microfilms are stored in fireproof vaults. They will be available even if the originals are damaged or lost.

American students of European history can now see, on microfilm, documents dating back to the time of King Henry VII of England. They can examine ancient manuscripts from the Vatican Library in Rome. A European student of American history can consult the records of the first United States Congress, or the results of the first United States Census of 1790. Each year, more old and rare material is transferred to microfilm.

Today's newspapers, printed on a kind of paper that deteriorates rapidly, are being copied on microfilm. Historians are already consulting microfilmed newspapers. Government records, too, are being preserved on microfilm, a "breakthrough" for historians of the present—and the future.

1. Newspapers today are printed on paper
   - a. impossible to destroy.
   - b. that deteriorates rapidly.
   - c. from old manuscripts.
   - d. made from microfilm.

2. The word in paragraph 1 that means *refer to for information* is

   _____ .

3. The words "which copies and reduces pages of printed or written matter" in

   paragraph 3 describe a photographic _____ .

4. While it is not directly stated, the article suggests that
   - a. rare books and documents are to be treasured.
   - b. all rare books must be kept in Vatican City.
   - c. most American students now own rare books.

5. To read microfilm, the user puts a reel
   - a. on a record.
   - b. in a machine.
   - c. inside a book.

6. On the whole, the article tells about
   - a. European students of American history.
   - b. documents belonging to King Henry VII.
   - c. preserving rare documents on microfilm.

7. Which statement does this article lead you to believe?
   - a. Microfilm is useful in many fields.
   - b. Only historians ever use microfilm.
   - c. No one reads newspapers on microfilm.

8. Why are rare books stored after microfilming?
   - a. They lose their value after microfilming.
   - b. Storage protects them from damage or theft.
   - c. The United States Census ordered this done.

9. Think about the concept for this group of articles. Which statement seems true
   both for the article and for the concept?
   - a. Today's historians use modern methods in research.
   - b. Microfilming documents goes back to King Henry VII.
   - c. As soon as documents are microfilmed, they are destroyed.

TUBMAN

DREW

WOODS

CHISHOLM

WHEATLEY

BANNEKER

MATZELIGER

Righting a Wrong

For centuries, history textbooks used in American schools neglected the role of black Americans in shaping history. Often, the books mentioned only George Washington Carver and Booker T. Washington as important Negroes in America's past. As a result, many Americans do not yet know about other black Americans who also contributed to America's past.

Older American history books did not mention Benjamin Banneker, an important figure of Colonial days. Although he was a scientist, mathematician, and writer, Benjamin Banneker is best known for his role in helping to plan the nation's capital. He was appointed by George Washington to serve on the committee that planned Washington, D.C.

In earlier days, students did not learn that Afro-American inventors developed hundreds of new ideas. An important inventor was Granville T. Woods. He invented the automatic air brake used on railroad trains. Another black inventor, Jan Matzeliger, invented a machine that combined the many separate steps of shoe manufacture. Today, a multimillion-dollar shoe company uses his invention.

Afro-Americans have also made important contributions to the field of medicine. In 1893, a black doctor, Dr. Daniel Hale Williams, performed the world's first successful open-heart surgery. In the 1940s, Dr. Charles Drew developed the first useful system of blood banks. Dr. Percy Julian helped develop drugs used to treat persons suffering from arthritis.

Today, history textbooks are changing. Increasingly, educators, authors, and publishers have produced some textbooks that recognize the part of Afro-Americans in our history. More books are being planned. In this modern age, Americans have come to realize that the record of their history is not complete without the major contributions of black people to American life.

1. Granville T. Woods invented the
   a. time machine.
   b. jet airplane.
   c. automatic air brake.
   d. automobile hand brake.

2. The word in paragraph 1 that means *paid no attention to* is

   _____ .

3. The words "an important figure of Colonial days" in paragraph 2 describe

   _____   _____ .

4. While it is not directly stated, the article suggests that
   a. students have always been aware of the role of Afro-Americans.
   b. a history textbook never omits any known historical facts.
   c. students have much to learn about the history of Afro-Americans.

5. A machine invented by Jan Matzeliger is used in
   a. the drug industry.
   b. television shows.
   c. shoe manufacture.

6. On the whole, the article tells about
   a. the important role of black people in American history.
   b. drugs that have been used to cure people of arthritis.
   c. the committee that helped plan the nation's capital.

7. Which statement does the article lead you to believe?
   a. The record of the black community is important to all Americans.
   b. There were only two important people in the black community.
   c. The black community was important only in the old Colonial days.

8. Why was Dr. Daniel Hale Williams' contribution so important?
   a. He was the first man to put blood in a bank system.
   b. He paved the way to successful open-heart surgery.
   c. He owned a multi-million dollar shoe company.

9. Think about the concept for this group of articles. Which statement seems true both for the article and for the concept?
   a. There were no important Afro-Americans as far back as Colonial days.
   b. Afro-Americans have always been recognized for their contributions.
   c. Afro-Americans must get recognition for their contributions to history.

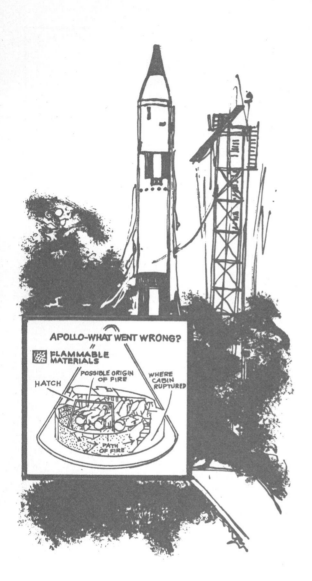

APOLLO—WHAT WENT WRONG?

FLAMMABLE MATERIALS

HATCH

POSSIBLE ORIGIN OF FIRE

WHERE CABIN RUPTURED

PATH OF FIRE

Safety in Space

The first major disaster of the United States space program took place at Cape Kennedy—on the ground.

On January 27, 1967, Virgil Grissom, Edward White, and Roger Chaffee were taking part in a training exercise that simulated a real flight. They wore space suits and helmets, and they were tightly sealed inside an Apollo space capsule.

Suddenly, fire blazed inside the capsule, and within twenty seconds it was a charred shell. The three men who had hoped to be the first Apollo astronauts died.

What went wrong? Experts who examined the burnt-out spacecraft guessed that faulty wiring had started a fire. The atmosphere inside the capsule had been pure oxygen at a pressure of 16 pounds per square inch. In that atmosphere, fire burns much faster and hotter than in air at normal pressure. Plastic storage nets and foam rubber pads had fed the blaze. Because of a hatch cover that took thirty seconds to open, the three astronauts had no chance to escape.

The tragedy shocked and saddened the nation. The scientists and engineers who had designed the spacecraft realized that mistakes had been made. Perhaps they had grown overconfident because the Mercury and Gemini programs had been so successful. Perhaps they had moved too fast, in an effort to keep the United States program ahead in space exploration.

The timetable for Apollo flights had to be set back. More time was allowed for testing, redesigning, and careful planning. All flammable materials inside the capsule were replaced with nonflammable materials. The slow-opening hatch cover was replaced with one that could be opened quickly.

The first manned Apollo spaceflight took place in October 1968. Two months later, *Apollo 8* carried three men safely around the moon and back.

1. The first major disaster in our space program happened
   a. in the ocean.
   b. on the ground.
   c. in outer space.
   d. on another planet.

2. The word in paragraph 2 that means *had the appearance of* is

   _____ .

3. The words "who had designed the spacecraft" in paragraph 5 describe the

   _____ and _____ .

4. While it is not directly stated, the article suggests that
   a. the death of three men resulted in new safety measures.
   b. it is impossible for anything to go wrong in a spacecraft.
   c. fire always burns slowly in an atmosphere of pure oxygen.

5. The timetable for Apollo flights had to be
   a. moved ahead.
   b. dropped.
   c. set back.

6. On the whole, the article tells about
   a. events following the death of three astronauts.
   b. the first manned Apollo spaceflight in October.
   c. the number of mistakes made by people in space.

7. Which statement does the article lead you to believe?
   a. It is important to put flammable materials in spacecraft.
   b. All spacecraft now contain slow-opening hatches hard to open.
   c. Spacecraft must improve as men learn more about space.

8. Why were mistakes made in our spacecraft?
   a. Our spacecraft were planned by foreign agents.
   b. Engineers and scientists refused to work together.
   c. Possibly we were overconfident and moved too fast.

9. Think about the concept for this group of articles. Which statement seems true both for the article and for the concept?
   a. Change is a continual process in space research.
   b. Space research makes no allowance for any changes.
   c. Our space program is fine just the way it is now.

Sharing Knowledge of Space

On October 4, 1957, the earth's first artificial satellite was rocketed into orbit. The satellite was the Russian *Sputnik I.* The date marked the beginning of the Space Age and the beginning of a "space race" between two nations, the United States and Russia.

Four months later, the United States placed a satellite named *Explorer I* in orbit.

On April 12, 1961, Yuri Gagarin of Russia became the first man to orbit the earth, in the spacecraft *Vostok I.* On February 20, 1962, United States astronaut John Glenn orbited the earth in the spacecraft *Friendship 7.*

After Glenn's flight, Chairman Nikita Khrushchev of the Soviet Union sent congratulations to President John F. Kennedy of the United States. President Kennedy answered by suggesting that Russia and the United States work together on certain kinds of space research. He proposed some projects that could be carried on cooperatively by scientists in the two countries. By working together and exchanging information, the two groups of scientists could avoid wasteful and expensive duplication of research.

In June 1962, representatives of Russia and the United States agreed on a plan for three cooperative research projects. One project involved research with communications satellites. Another called for exchange of information obtained from weather satellites. The third project was joint mapping of the earth's magnetic field.

The project concerning exchange of weather information progressed most rapidly. In 1964, a direct line was set up between meteorological centers in Moscow and in Washington, D.C. Twenty-four hours a day, this line transmits information about the state of the atmosphere. Some of the information is obtained from weather satellites. The shared information makes possible more accurate weather forecasts in both nations.

1. The spacecraft *Vostok I* was put into orbit by
   a. Poland.   c. Germany.
   b. Russia.   d. Rumania.

2. The word in paragraph 6 that means *having to do with the atmosphere, and particularly weather* is _____ .

3. The words "that could be carried on cooperatively" in paragraph 4 describe some _____ .

4. While it is not directly stated, the article suggests that
   a. scientists of many nations want to work together.
   b. Nikita Khrushchev of Russia was a famous scientist.
   c. scientists will never learn to pool their knowledge.

5. A direct line was set up in 1964 between
   a. Pittsburgh, Pa., and Warsaw.
   b. Baltimore, Md., and Leningrad.
   c. Washington, D.C., and Moscow.

6. On the whole, the article tells about
   a. President John F. Kennedy of the United States.
   b. the cooperation between nations on space projects.
   c. using satellites to map the earth's magnetic field.

7. Which statement does the article lead you to believe?
   a. Cooperative research projects could help nations in many areas.
   b. Weather forecasts force nations to cooperate in science centers.
   c. It is not true that scientists sometimes duplicate research.

8. Why did President Kennedy want American and Russian scientists to work together?
   a. He wanted to avoid wasteful and expensive duplication of research.
   b. He wanted to find out if Russian scientists understood English.
   c. He wanted to see if scientists could work together in outer space.

9. Think about the concept for this group of articles. Which statement seems true both for the article and for the concept?
   a. No nation will ever share scientific information with another.
   b. Nations must plan to work together for the good of all.
   c. Nations do much better when they keep all science secret.

Fish for the Future

The salmon is one of our most valuable fish. It offers us food, sport, and profit. Every year commercial fishing results in a harvest of over a billion pounds of salmon from the sea. Hundreds of thousands of salmon are caught each year by eager sports fishers.

In autumn, the rivers of the Northwestern United States come alive with salmon. The salmon have left the ocean and are on their yearly run upriver to spawn. Yet today, there are far fewer salmon than ever before, because the salmon population has suffered from many perils of the modern age.

Water pollution has killed many salmon by robbing them of oxygen. Overfishing has further decreased their numbers. Dams are another danger, because they block migration paths. Fish ladders, made up of stepped pools, have been built so that salmon can swim safely over the dams. But young salmon swimming to the ocean have trouble finding the ladders. Often they fall to their deaths over the dam or are killed in giant hydroelectric turbines.

So that America will continue to have plenty of salmon, conservationists have planned several ways to increase the salmon population. Conservation officials have had some success raising salmon in hatcheries and stocking salmon rivers with them. Salmon are also being introduced into new areas. In 1966, hundreds of thousands of young coho salmon were planted in streams off Lake Michigan. The adults were expected to migrate to the lake and feed upon an undesirable fish called the alewife. The cohos thrived so well on the alewives in Lake Michigan that

cohos are being planted in other Great Lakes.

Thanks to the foresight and planning of conservationists, the valuable salmon should be around American shores, rivers, and lakes for a long time to come.

1. The rivers of Northwestern United States come alive with salmon in
      a. autumn.   c. summer.
      b. spring.   d. winter.

2. The word in the last paragraph that means *the act of looking ahead* is

   _____.

3. The words "an undesirable fish" in paragraph 4 describe the

   _____.

4. While it is not directly stated, the article suggests that
      a. salmon are found only in fresh waters.
      b. there is no salmon fishing in the United States.
      c. many people enjoy eating salmon.

5. Water pollution robs salmon of
      a. plants.
      b. ladders.
      c. oxygen.

6. On the whole, the article tells about
      a. stepped pools in some dams.
      b. conserving a valuable fish.
      c. giant hydroelectric turbines.

7. Which statement does the article lead you to believe?
      a. Salmon cannot spawn in the ocean.
      b. There are giants in most turbines.
      c. Dams are built of migration blocks.

8. Why were young coho salmon planted in streams near Lake Michigan?
      a. Conservationists hoped to reduce the number of salmon.
      b. This was a better place for them than the fish hatcheries.
      c. The adults were supposed to help get rid of the alewives.

9. Think about the concept for this group of articles. Which statement seems true both for the article and for the concept?
      a. Conservationists have many plans to preserve our animal life.
      b. Conservationists are people who build ladders in pools.
      c. Conservationists are only interested in salmon as food.

Pollution: Everybody's Business

Humans live in a natural environment, just as plants and animals do. But there is a difference. Humans have changed the environment to suit their needs.

Over past centuries, people have cut down forests and plowed up prairies. They have dammed up some rivers and dug new courses for others. They have hunted some kinds of animals into extinction and increased the number of other kinds.

Since the beginning of the Industrial Age, humans have changed the environment more rapidly than ever before. Cities, factories, and vehicles have produced millions of tons of poisonous wastes. These wastes have been carelessly released into streams, lakes, and into the air.

Into the streams and lakes went raw sewage from cities and poisonous chemicals used by factories. Into the air went smoke, factory fumes, and poisonous gases from auto and truck exhausts.

Millions of fish, birds, land animals, and plants have already been killed by air and water pollution. Air pollution contributes to cancer, heart disease, and respiratory diseases in humans.

The nation needed laws requiring cities and factories to purify their waste products before dumping them into streams and lakes. Industry needed ways to purify gases before they were released from vehicle exhausts and factories.

In 1966, Congress voted 3½ billion dollars to help American cities build new and better sewage disposal plants. Another 60 million was voted for research into better ways of industrial water disposal. States were required to set up plans to reduce water pollution. In 1968, a new law required all new autos to have devices that reduced exhaust fumes.

People have realized at last that they must be better housekeepers within the environment. Otherwise, someday there may be no fresh air left to breathe and no fresh water to drink.

FIND THE ANSWERS

1. Humans have changed their environment more rapidly since the
   a. Ice Age.   c. Pennsylvanian Age.
   b. Bronze Age.   d. Industrial Age.

2. The word in paragraph 2 that means *no longer existing* or *dying out* is

   _____ .

3. The words "into streams, lakes, and into the air" in paragraph 3 tell about the

   _____ .

4. While it is not directly stated, the article suggests that
   a. animals should be hunted until they are extinct.
   b. some animals have disappeared from earth forever.
   c. hunters help increase the number of wild animals.

5. A new law required new autos to have devices that reduced
   a. respiration.
   b. exhaust fumes.
   c. sand dunes.

6. On the whole, the article tells about
   a. the effects of pollution on our environment.
   b. animals who live in an artificial environment.
   c. the proper way to introduce poisonous gases.

7. Which statement does this article lead you to believe?
   a. People have always used the natural resources wisely.
   b. People have been very wasteful of the natural resources.
   c. People do not need fresh air to breathe or fresh water to drink.

8. Why did Congress vote 3½ billion dollars for American cities?
   a. They wanted to help American cities build bigger wastepaper baskets.
   b. They felt American cities did not have enough sewage for disposal.
   c. They wanted the cities to build new and better sewage disposal plants.

9. Think about the concept for this group of articles. Which statement seems true both for the article and for the concept?
   a. Proper planning may still save the natural environment of humans.
   b. Housekeepers are better able to plan than conservationists.
   c. People cannot get cancer without the help of air pollution.

The Governor's Mistake

In 1900, a British governor in West Africa made a mistake that started a small war. The governor demanded that Ashanti tribe members surrender a golden stool that belonged to the tribe. He thought that the stool was a kind of throne. He believed he could show his authority over the tribe if he had the stool.

But the governor had made an error, for the stool was much more than a throne to the Ashanti. To them, it was a sacred relic that contained the spirit of the tribe. The stool was so sacred that even the Ashanti chief could not sit on it.

Rather than surrender the stool, the tribe members hid it. Shortly afterward, British soldiers moved in and fighting began. Many of the Ashanti were killed. If the governor had only realized the true meaning of the stool to the Ashanti, he might not have demanded it from them.

The war might have been avoided if the governor had first consulted an anthropologist. Anthropologists are scientists who study people and how they have lived. Some anthropologists make special studies of the customs and beliefs of different societies.

Today, the governments of advanced nations are giving aid to underdeveloped nations. In some cases, these nations want to make a quick, giant step from tribal ways to advanced ways of doing things. Yet tribal ways sometimes conflict with progress.

With advice from anthropologists, the United States has planned foreign-aid programs that fit in with the customs of nations that are not yet industrialized. For example, anthropologists are helping young men and women of the Peace Corps understand and show respect for the customs and beliefs of emerging nations. In that way, their people can take the "giant step" they desire with minimum confusion and misunderstanding.

1. The governor could have avoided war by consulting an
    a. anthropologist.   c. anarchist.
    b. astro-physicist.   d. allergist.

2. The word in paragraph 2 that means *an object remaining from the past* is

    _____ .

3. The words "a kind of throne" in paragraph 1 describe the _____ .

4. While it is not directly stated, the article suggests that
    a. symbols have different meanings for different people.
    b. a throne is the only kind of symbol people respect.
    c. the governor understood the true meaning of the symbol.

5. Anthropologists today are helping young men and women of the
    a. Marine Corps.
    b. Peace Corps.
    c. Apple Cores.

6. On the whole, the article tells about
    a. the need to understand the customs and beliefs of different societies.
    b. the importance of an Ashanti chief in the governor's society.
    c. the need to advance the confusion of anthropologists in our society.

7. Which statement does this article lead you to believe?
    a. The transition to modern times is very difficult for some people.
    b. Emerging nations have no problems fitting into the modern world.
    c. Tribe members who want to be modern must hide their sacred relics.

8. Why did the governor want the golden stool of the Ashanti tribesmen?
    a. He thought it would help him show his authority over the tribe.
    b. He thought the golden stool did not belong to these tribe members.
    c. He thought the stool was a sacred relic belonging to Europeans.

9. Think about the concept for this group of articles. Which statement seems true both for the article and for the concept?
    a. No one can ever learn the customs and beliefs of other nations.
    b. It is only important to understand the customs of your own country.
    c. People now try to understand the customs of those they wish to help.

The Many Voices of India

About fourteen major languages and several hundred dialects are spoken in India. As a result, the Indian government has enormous problems in trying to knit together as a nation the many different tribal and religious groups in India.

Delegates attend national conferences and may not always understand what the other delegates say. Radio networks broadcast the news in fourteen different languages. Yet there are many people in India who don't understand any of them.

While India was a part of the British Empire, English was the official language of the government. Yet only about 2 percent of the Indian people spoke English. When India gained its independence in 1947, the country's leaders wanted to drop English for a language of India's own. They chose Hindi, which is understood by about 40 percent of the people. The Hindi-speaking people live mostly in northern India. Most of the people of southern India did not understand Hindi. They resented this choice. In some of India's twenty-seven states, bloody riots were started by groups wanting to continue using their own languages.

In 1956, the Indian government announced a plan for reorganizing India's twenty-seven states into fourteen new states. These new states corresponded roughly to India's major language areas. Each state could adopt its own major language for official use within the state. Later, two more states were formed to accommodate large groups who didn't want to use the languages adopted for their areas.

In 1967, the government voted to continue using English as an "associate" language along with Hindi for official business. The government backed a plan by which all Indian children would learn three languages: English, Hindi, and a local language. Until then, English may serve as a link to bind them together.

1. When India was part of the British Empire, the official language was
   a. Hindi.
   b. French.
   c. Chinese.
   d. English.

2. The word in paragraph 1 that means *separate forms of a language, each belonging to an area or group of people* is _____.

3. The words "as an associate language" in the last paragraph describe the word _____.

4. While it is not directly stated, the article suggests that
   a. everyone in India can speak and understand the English language.
   b. language can never be a real barrier among the people of India.
   c. it is hard for the Indian people to communicate with each other.

5. The Hindi-speaking people live mostly in
   a. northern India.
   b. western Mexico.
   c. eastern China.

6. On the whole, the article tells about
   a. reorganizing official business in Hindi.
   b. the confusion of languages in India.
   c. the problem Indians have in knitting.

7. Which statement does this article lead you to believe?
   a. Indians feel all their problems can be solved by the English.
   b. India has many problems that will take a long time to solve.
   c. The Indian government has very few problems left to solve.

8. Why did the people of southern India resent the choice of Hindi?
   a. It sounded too much like English.
   b. Most of them did not understand it.
   c. They preferred to speak in Swahili.

9. Think about the concept for this group of articles. Which statement seems true both for the article and for the concept?
   a. India should progress more quickly when it has a common language.
   b. The Indian government is not interested in using a common language.
   c. Indian children are not expected to learn their own language.

Prosperity Comes to the Poorhouse

The Spanish name *Puerto Rico* means "rich port" in English, but in 1940 the island was called the poorhouse of the Caribbean.

A possession of the United States since 1898, Puerto Rico has many mountains and is densely populated. There is little land for farming, and heavy rains erode the soil. Yet until 1940, the island's economy was based on the growing of sugarcane, coffee, and tobacco.

There was little industry. Nothing useful could be mined, and few tourists came to enjoy the beautiful beaches because there were no good hotels.

In the early 1940s, far-sighted Puerto Rican and United States leaders planned "Operation Bootstrap" to improve the island's economy. With technical and financial help from the United States government, Puerto Rico attacked its problems in several different ways.

Tax benefits and low-rent buildings were offered to investors who would start factories in Puerto Rico. To prepare Puerto Ricans for jobs in the factories, an adult education program emphasizing English and trade skills was started.

A land distribution program broke up large estates and created more small farms. Farmers were urged to plant more different crops, while dairy farming and cattle raising were encouraged.

To lure tourists, the Puerto Rican government built one modern resort hotel. The island soon became a popular vacation place. Investors soon built many more hotels.

Was "Operation Bootstrap" successful? Between 1940 and 1960, the yearly income of the average Puerto Rican rose from $121 to $740. Total income from farming rose from 70 million dollars to nearly 200 million dollars. Income from manufacturing rose from 27 million dollars to 384 million dollars.

There is still unemployment in Puerto Rico, and wages there are lower than in continental United States. But the "poorhouse" has become the wealthiest of the Caribbean islands.

1. The name *Puerto Rico* in English means
   a. poor sport.   c. army fort.
   b. rich port.   d. red quart.

2. The word in paragraph 5 that means *pointing out the importance of* is

   _____.

3. The words "poorhouse of the Caribbean" in paragraph 1 refer to the

   _____.

4. While it is not directly stated, the article suggests that
   a. investors were encouraged to start many new farms.
   b. all the people of Puerto Rico are still farmers.
   c. there are many skilled workers in Puerto Rico today.

5. The Puerto Rican government built one modern resort to
   a. lure tourists.
   b. trap traders.
   c. house cattle.

6. On the whole, the article tells about
   a. the right place to build a new poorhouse.
   b. government officials who wear bootstraps.
   c. the fight to improve Puerto Rico's economy.

7. Which statement does this article lead you to believe?
   a. The income of the Puerto Ricans has dropped steadily since 1940.
   b. The level of income in Puerto Rico does not matter to anyone.
   c. The level of income in Puerto Rico will continue to improve.

8. Why did leaders of Puerto Rico and the United States plan "Operation Bootstrap"?
   a. They wanted to improve the island's economy.
   b. They had an over production of bootstraps.
   c. They wanted to reduce the island's efficiency.

9. Think about the concept for this group of articles. Which statement seems true both for the article and for the concept?
   a. Education and planning will build a good future for Puerto Ricans.
   b. Education is not important for people who have very low incomes.
   c. Adult education programs in Puerto Rico emphasize Latin and Greek.

COMMON MARKET HEADQUARTERS

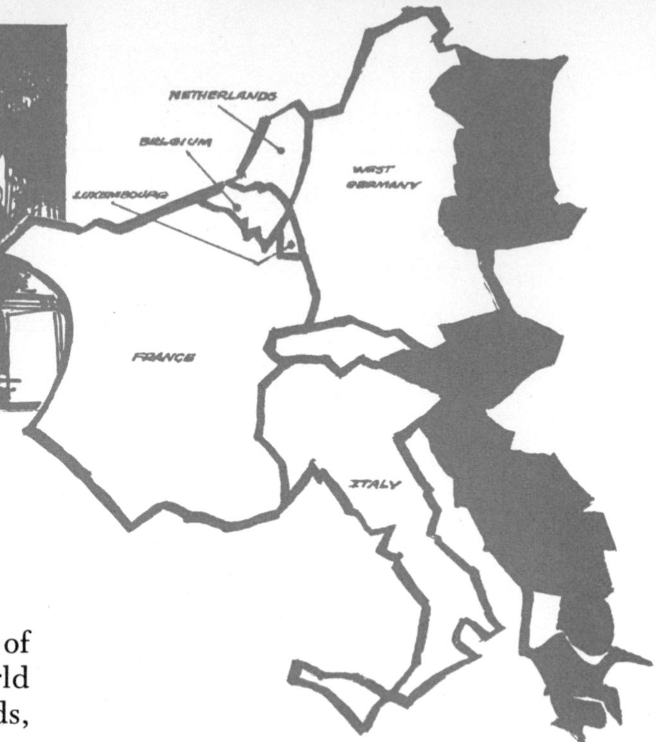

Map labels: NETHERLANDS, BELGIUM, LUXEMBOURG, WEST GERMANY, FRANCE, ITALY

The Walls Come Down

Western Europe is a patchwork of nations that seem small by New World standards. Belgium, the Netherlands, and Luxembourg are, combined, only a little larger than West Virginia. France, which looks large on the map of Europe, is smaller than Texas.

These small nations have had a long history of wars over boundaries, jealousies, and competition. But recent times have been different. Some barriers are crumbling, and national leaders are learning to work together for the common good of all.

When World War II ended, most European industry was in ruins and the nations were very poor. National leaders believed that economic recovery would be speeded if manufacturers could buy and sell freely across national boundaries. They made plans for a cooperative economic union that became the European Common Market. Representatives of six nations met in Rome, in March 1957, to sign the agreement creating this union. The six partner nations were Belgium, the Netherlands, Luxembourg, France, Italy, and West Germany.

The barriers began to come down. First to go were the different import duties that the six nations had been charging each other. Raw materials, manufactured goods, money, and skilled workers soon began to move more freely from one member nation to another. Later, the Common Market nations began to charge a common import duty to the products of all non-member nations. This replaced the range of different import duties that had been charged.

In ten years, the value of goods manufactured by the six member nations increased 52 percent. Exports to non-member nations doubled. Consumer spending within member nations doubled. Trade between the member nations tripled.

Good planning by farsighted leaders helped bring new wealth to these six war-damaged nations. Today, the European Common Market is a strong competitor in world trade.

120

1. France is smaller than
   a. Toledo.
   b. Toronto.
   c. Texas.
   d. Tampa.

2. The word in paragraph 4 that means *things standing in the way* is

   _____ .

3. The words "wars over boundaries" in paragraph 2 refer to the small nations'

   _____ .

4. While it is not directly stated, the article suggests that
   a. wars were destroying the economy of small nations.
   b. there are not enough small nations in Europe.
   c. arguments between nations are best settled by trade barriers.

5. The cooperative economic union that was planned became the
   a. European Copper Market.
   b. European Common Market.
   c. European Preferred Market.

6. On the whole, the article tells about
   a. developing economic cooperation among six nations.
   b. creating trade barriers to help economic recovery.
   c. ruining the economy across six national boundaries.

7. Which statement does this article lead you to believe?
   a. The six war-damaged nations are the world's weakest competitors.
   b. Members of a cooperative economic union cannot compete for trade.
   c. In order to help themselves, nations are helping each other.

8. Why did representatives of six nations meet in Rome?
   a. They met to sign an agreement creating an economic union.
   b. They met to create new economic barriers in Europe.
   c. They met to start charging each other import duties.

9. Think about the concept for this group of articles. Which statement seems true both for the article and for the concept?
   a. As they grow, these nations may learn to cooperate in other matters.
   b. The nations of Europe wish to become part of the United States.
   c. The continent of Europe consists of only six war-damaged nations.

An Eye in the Sky

Mapmakers have to work fast to keep up with rapid changes on the face of the earth. New highways and bridges are built. Dams form new lakes. Almost overnight, new housing and factories fan out around large cities. To be useful, maps must be revised constantly to show these changes.

Mapmakers have used a handy tool that helps them keep up with the changes. Aerial photography quickly and accurately collects information about the face of the earth.

Mapmaking planes carry cameras that point straight down. Each photograph shows one small, square part of the earth's surface, but the camera takes many overlapping photographs as the plane flies back and forth over the area to be mapped. Later, these photos are carefully trimmed and fitted together.

An aerial camera can see some things not visible from ground level. It can look down through water and map submarine canyons and the limits of the continental shelf. It can map rock formations not apparent on the surface. With special film, it can spot where water or oil deposits may lie under the surface.

In the 1970s, a new device was launched into orbit almost 600 miles above the earth. It was a satellite called Landsat 1; it was joined a few years later by Landsat 2.

The unusual part of the satellites' job was to give a picture of the 48 states without using regular cameras. Landsat used a device called a scanner. With a kind of swinging mirror and a telescope, the scanner focused special light waves and sent the signals back to earth. The information was put together with the help of a computer. This gave a much clearer picture than photographs taken by airplanes at lower altitudes.

1. Some cameras are mounted on
   - a. satellites.
   - b. Saturn.
   - c. fortifications.
   - d. meteorologists.

2. The word in paragraph 3 that means *covering and stretching beyond* is

   _____.

3. The word "carefully" in paragraph 3 describes

   _____ and _____.

4. While it is not directly stated, the article suggests that
   - a. old maps gave too much information.
   - b. old maps are better than new ones.
   - c. old maps were not completely accurate.

5. Cameras in space can send photographs to earth showing
   - a. whole continents.
   - b. rock formations.
   - c. eyes up in the sky.

6. On the whole, the article tells about
   - a. new housing and factories around large cities.
   - b. rock formations that show where water may lie.
   - c. aerial methods used in mapmaking.

7. Which statement does this article lead you to believe?
   - a. The aerial camera is used to make automatic mapping machines.
   - b. Aerial views have given us a new picture of our earth.
   - c. The aerial camera answers all of our questions about earth.

8. Why was the satellites' job so unusual?
   - a. They helped to trim the maps carefully.
   - b. They gave us a picture of the 48 states without using a camera.
   - c. They helped to find new rock formations.

9. Think about the concept for this group of articles. Which statement seems true both for the article and for the concept?
   - a. Modern mapmakers have to travel a lot.
   - b. Modern mapmaking requires modern methods.
   - c. Modern mapmakers use prehistoric maps.

harvesting as lumber or pulpwood. But a tree crop can be a good investment for a landowner or farmer, since trees will grow on the parts of his land where ordinary crops will not grow.

Trees do much more than provide lumber for home building. They provide raw materials for making paper, plastics, synthetics, turpentine, and other products. Even more important, trees protect the nation's water supply by holding back erosion and keeping water in the soil.

America once had huge natural forests. To start their farms, pioneers cleared many trees. Later, logging crews employed by lumber companies moved into other forests. They cut all the valuable trees, and then moved on.

There were few efforts to protect our forests or to plant new ones until the beginning of the present century. Then, together with forest experts, government officials, and landowners, the lumber companies began planning to support the planting of new forests. The American Tree Farm System, begun during World War II, is one of the plans that grew out of this cooperation.

Landowners who wish to establish tree farms can get help from a professional, state-employed forester, or from an association of lumber companies. They can get advice on what kind of trees to plant and how to care for them. Landowners must protect their trees by keeping grazing animals away and by removing dead or diseased trees. They must keep replanting, so that young trees are growing at all times to replace those ready for cutting.

Some tree farms are small woodlots. Others cover thousands of acres. All together, they are of great value to the United States and its people.

A Harvest for the Future

Unlike many plants, trees grow slowly. Thirty to eighty years are necessary before a tree grows to the right size for

1. For a tree to grow large enough for harvesting may take
   - a. eleven to fifteen months.
   - c. ten to twenty days.
   - b. five to six years.
   - d. thirty to eighty years.

2. The word in paragraph 2 that means *the wearing away of the earth* is

   _____ .

3. The words "unlike many plants" in paragraph 1 refer to _____ .

4. While it is not directly stated, the article suggests that
   - a. trees can be destroyed in many ways.
   - b. trees were preserved by our pioneers.
   - c. huge forests can be found everywhere.

5. A landowner who wants to start a tree farm can get help from a
   - a. harvester.
   - b. foreigner.
   - c. forester.

6. On the whole, the article tells about
   - a. making finished products from raw materials.
   - b. planting and protecting our valuable trees.
   - c. an association formed by lumber companies.

7. Which statement does this article lead you to believe?
   - a. The American Tree Farm System was begun by early pioneers.
   - b. Landowners must belong to an association of lumber companies.
   - c. Many different people are concerned with saving the land.

8. Why did pioneers clear the trees from some forests?
   - a. They needed clear land to start their farms.
   - b. They didn't like the way the trees were growing.
   - c. The pioneers needed the exercise to stay strong.

9. Think about the concept for this group of articles. Which statement seems true both for the article and for the concept?
   - a. Grazing animals cannot do any harm to young growing plants.
   - b. People have always understood the danger of clearing too much land.
   - c. People today have a better understanding of their environment.

More Than Flood Control

The Tennessee River Basin is an area of 40,000 square miles that includes parts of seven states, from Kentucky to Alabama. In the early 1930s, the Tennessee basin was a land of floods, eroded farms, and cut-over forests. There were few industries, unemployment was widespread, and most people in the area were very poor.

In 1933 something happened to change all that. A government agency—the Tennessee Valley Authority—was formed to put the river to work helping the people.

The heart of the TVA plan was the building of thirty dams on the Tennessee River and its tributaries. The dams served many different purposes. They provided a deeper channel, so that freight barges and other boats could use the river. They generated low-priced electric power. They prevented floods and they formed new lakes that could be used for boating and fishing.

The TVA plan went beyond merely putting the river to work. Farmers were taught better ways of plowing to control erosion. They were provided with low-cost fertilizers. Seedling trees were planted to replace the cut-over forests.

Within a few years, the whole area benefited. New factories were built to take advantage of the water transportation and electric power. The factories provided jobs. They paid taxes that were used in turn to build better schools and better roads. New parks and boat docks brought visitors to the lakes, providing still more new sources of income. Today, those seedling trees have grown into valuable forests.

The TVA plan was a long-range plan that went far beyond solving the problem of flood control. It improved the land and restored much of its beauty. It raised the economy of an entire area.

1. The Tennessee River Basin includes parts of seven states from
    a. Canarsie to Arizona.   c. Canada to Alaska.
    b. Kentucky to Alabama.   d. Kansas to Alabama.

2. The word in paragraph 3 that means *streams that flow into a main river system*

   is _____ .

3. The words "an entire area" in paragraph 6 tell about an _____ .

4. While it is not directly stated, the article suggests that
    a. sometimes people can make nature work for them.
    b. the natural environment can never be changed.
    c. it is wrong to put a river to work for people.

5. The whole area benefited
    a. in less than a month.
    b. within a few years.
    c. after twelve days.

6. On the whole, the article tells about
    a. the benefits that resulted from the Tennessee Valley Authority.
    b. the poor planning that was caused by a Tennessee River Authority.
    c. different government agencies and the tasks they perform.

7. Which statement does this article lead you to believe?
    a. Many different studies were necessary for the TVA plan.
    b. It is not up to people to beautify the land they use.
    c. It is not important for land to be improved at this time.

8. Why were farmers able to control erosion?
    a. The rains stopped for several years.
    b. They had low-priced electric power.
    c. They learned better ways of plowing.

9. Think about the concept for this group of articles. Which statement seems true both for the article and for the concept?
    a. Good planning has many wide-range benefits.
    b. It is better for things to happen naturally.
    c. Too many changes are not good for people.

Conquering a Mighty River

The great Mississippi River has served well the people who live near it. But it has also been their enemy. From time to time, heavy rains or melting snows have caused the river to swell and overflow its banks. In the past, such floods have taken many lives. They have destroyed millions of dollars in crops and property.

Planning ways to control floods is the task of the United States Corps of Engineers. In the 1800s, the engineers tried to wall in the river downstream by building a levee that was larger than the Great Wall of China. But after a disastrous flood in 1927, people came to realize that much more flood control was needed. Using giant barges and huge suction dredges that could scoop the earth from the river bed, the Corps of Engineers then set to work on enormous flood control projects.

The engineers built new levees. These levees were from 30 to 50 feet high. They extended up the Mississippi and its tributaries for more than 3,000 miles. In some places, the Mississippi was shallow and flooded easily. The engineers dredged out these shallow places until they were at least 12 feet deep. They also built canals which could carry floodwaters away from the river and into the Gulf of Mexico. Dams were built on the Mississippi's tributaries to hold back excess water.

In the past, the Mississippi was forever shifting its banks. But south of Cairo, Illinois, the engineers have been preserving the river's banks with levees built of earth reinforced with metal cable and mesh. It is planned that the river's channel should be permanently fixed from Cairo to Baton Rouge, Louisiana. The mighty Mississippi may be conquered.

1. In the 1800s, engineers built a levee larger than the
      a. tributaries.   c. 3,000 miles.
      b. length of the river.   d. Great Wall of China.

2. The word in paragraph 2 that means *bringing great misfortune* is

   _____ .

3. The words "swell and overflow its banks" in paragraph 1 tell about the

   _____ .

4. While it is not directly stated, the article suggests that
      a. flood control is a simple thing to accomplish.
      b. engineers do not know how to work on a river.
      c. the Mississippi is not yet fully controlled.

5. In some places, the Mississippi was
      a. shallow.
      b. shrunken.
      c. silent.

6. On the whole, the article tells about
      a. reinforcing levees with metal cables.
      b. building canals on the Gulf of Mexico.
      c. controlling floods along the Mississippi.

7. Which statement does this article lead you to believe?
      a. Someday people may not fear the Mississippi.
      b. The Mississippi never caused any severe damage.
      c. No one has ever lost a life when a river has flooded.

8. Why were dams built on the Mississippi's tributaries?
      a. They helped to fill the Mississippi with water.
      b. The dams were built to hold back excess water.
      c. Dams look better when built on the tributaries.

9. Think about the concept for this group of articles. Which statement seems true both for the article and for the concept?
      a. Technical knowledge will not help today's engineers at all.
      b. Technical knowledge will help engineers reach their goal.
      c. Anybody can engineer a flood control project to stop floods.

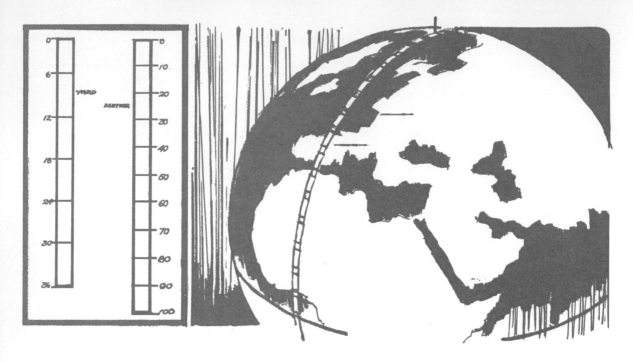

How Long Is a Meter?

The search for standards of accurate measurement has been going on for a long time. Today, accurate measurement is more important than ever before. The size of parts for precision machines and scientific instruments must be controlled carefully. A mistake of one-millionth of an inch in the parts of a spacecraft gyroscope is costly. It could cause a spacecraft aimed at the moon to miss by 1,000 miles.

Ideal standards of measurement are based on things in the natural world that do not change. Such standards can be copied accurately in different parts of the world, at different times.

French scientists were thinking along this line when, in 1799, they decided on the meter as a new unit of length. A meter was one ten-millionth of the distance between the north pole and the equator. The first standard meter was measured along a line fixed between Dunkirk, Belgium, and Barcelona, Spain.

The new meter proved a handy unit for measuring length. But making metal bars an exact meter long by computing one-fourth of the earth's circumference and then dividing by 10 million proved awkward. It was easier to make accurate meter bars by comparing them with a master unit. The master unit was a meter bar made of a platinum-iridium alloy. From 1889 until 1960, this bar served as the standard for all other meter bars.

In 1960, the General Conference of Weights and Measures met in Paris and decided on a new standard meter better suited to modern needs. This space-age meter is measured by the radiation of an atom of krypton, which is one of the 104 elements. The new standard measures the meter about a hundred times more accurately than the old standard. In addition, it can be accurately copied at any time, in any part of the world.

FIND THE ANSWERS

1. The first standard meter was measured along a line fixed between
   - a. Dunkirk and Barcelona.
   - b. Paris and Belgium.
   - c. Barcelona and Spain.
   - d. the pole and New York.

2. The word in paragraph 4 that means *figuring by arithmetic* is

   _____ .

3. The words "which is one of the 104 elements" in the last paragraph describe

   _____ .

4. While it is not directly stated, the article suggests that
   - a. measurements cannot be based on things in the natural world.
   - b. French scientists decided the old standards were the best.
   - c. modern needs require that measurements be very accurate.

5. It was easier to make accurate meter bars by
   - a. copying standards around the world.
   - b. daily measurements of the equator.
   - c. comparing them with a master unit.

6. On the whole, the article tells about
   - a. dividing the earth's circumference.
   - b. establishing a standard measure of length.
   - c. the 104 elements.

7. Which statement does this article lead you to believe?
   - a. Only one-fourth of the earth's circumference can be measured.
   - b. Mistakes in calculation can have serious effects on many things.
   - c. Standard meters are impossible to measure in modern times.

8. Why is a mistake of one-millionth of an inch in a gyroscope costly?
   - a. It can cause an astronaut to lose his spacecraft.
   - b. It can make a spacecraft miss its mark by 1,000 miles.
   - c. Industry pays for making precision machines by the inch.

9. Think about the concept for this group of articles. Which statement seems true both for the article and for the concept?
   - a. The Conference could not decide upon a new standard.
   - b. It is too difficult to measure radiation from an atom.
   - c. Scientists planned the new standard of measurement.

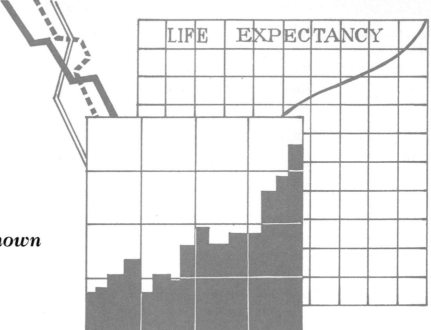

Guessing the Unknown

Suppose you had nothing better to do than flip a coin one million times. If you kept careful records of the million flips, your records would be called statistics. From your statistics, you might say, "A coin flipped a million times will come up heads about half the time." Your statement would be based on the Theory of Probability.

The Theory of Probability predicts only general truths. It does not predict single facts. For example, just because a coin lands heads up once does not mean that it will land tails up the next time. But the greater the number of times the coin is flipped, the greater the probability that half of the time the coin will land heads up.

Science and business often depend on the Theory of Probability. For instance, life insurance companies would like to know how long each insured person will live. The Theory of Probability allows some general predictions. From life-span statistics, an insurance company can predict about how many people in different companies will die each year at a certain age.

To draw up life-span statistics and set fair rates, insurance companies employ mathematicians called actuaries. An actuary must revise the statistics constantly, because life-spans are affected by many different things. In 1900, for example, the average life-span for a baby born in the United States was estimated at 47 years. Improved medical care increased the estimate to 70.2 years in 1961.

The person who buys life insurance is planning ahead. Actuaries must depend on accurate statistics and the Theory of Probability to plan even further ahead. In that way, life insurance companies can set fair rates for the buyers and make a fair profit from the insurance they sell.

FIND THE ANSWERS

1. Insurance companies employ mathematicians called
   - a. actuaries.
   - b. activists.
   - c. astrologists.
   - d. aviaries.

2. The word in paragraph 2 that means *foretell* is _____ .

3. The words "To draw up life-span statistics and set fair rates" in paragraph 4 refer to the _____ .

4. While it is not directly stated, the article suggests that
   - a. a person's life-span may depend on the age in which he or she lives.
   - b. insurance companies can accurately predict anyone's future.
   - c. your life-span depends on how many times you can flip a coin.

5. In 1900, the life-span for a new-born baby was
   - a. 99 years.
   - b. 70.2 years.
   - c. 47 years.

6. On the whole, the article tells about
   - a. using the Theory of Probability in a business.
   - b. actuaries who revise their statistics now and then.
   - c. improved medical care in the United States in 1900.

7. Which statement does this article lead you to believe?
   - a. More people reach old age in today's world.
   - b. The Theory of Probability keeps people alive.
   - c. Insurance companies are against medical care.

8. Why was the life-span estimate increased in 1961?
   - a. It increased the insurance companies' profits.
   - b. Actuaries made better guesses about life-spans.
   - c. Improved medical care increased the estimate.

9. Think about the concept for this group of articles. Which statement seems true both for the article and for the concept?
   - a. The Theory of Probability predicts only single facts.
   - b. The insurance business is built on planned predictions.
   - c. Statistics cannot be based on the life-span of people.

Traveling on Air

For many years, inventors dreamed of an all-purpose vehicle that would skim lightly over water. A cushion of compressed air would support the vehicle above the water surface.

Some inventors believed that the all-purpose vehicle would resemble an upside-down bathtub, with a hole in the top and a powerful fan inside. Air forced downward by the fan would raise the vehicle above any surface. On top of the hull, an ordinary propeller would move the craft forward. On rivers, lakes, and oceans, the craft could move much faster than an ordinary ship, whose speed is limited by the friction of water.

The first operating air-cushion vehicle (ACV) was built in the 1930s by a Finnish engineer, Toivo Kaario. But there was one serious problem. Because much of the high-pressure air from the fan leaked out from under the hull, an enormous amount of engine power was needed to raise Kaario's ACV. As a result, the first ACV was impractical and uneconomical.

In 1955, a British engineer named Christopher Cockerell planned an ACV called the Hovercraft. The air jets angled inward, resulting in an "air seal" that kept about 60 percent of the air from leaking out. The angled air jets gave Cockerell's ACV more lift on less power.

The first Hovercraft was launched in 1959. By 1965, two 15-passenger Hovercrafts were ferrying passengers across San Francisco Bay. Later 38-passenger Hovercrafts were operating in Scotland, Germany, and Norway.

In 1968, a 250-passenger Hovercraft began passenger service across the English Channel. Ordinary ferryboats take about two and a half hours to cross the 26-mile-wide Channel. The new Hovercraft, gliding along on its cushion of air, crosses in 35 minutes.

1. In 1968, a 250-passenger Hovercraft began passenger service across
    - a. the Mississippi River.
    - c. the English Channel.
    - b. the San Francisco Bay.
    - d. the Atlantic Ocean.

2. The word in paragraph 2 that means *look like* or *be similar to* is

    _____ .

3. The words "gliding along on its cushion of air" in the last paragraph describe

    the new _____ .

4. While it is not directly stated, the article suggests that
    - a. ferryboats ride on compressed air over water.
    - b. a Hovercraft ride may be smoother than a ferryboat ride.
    - c. Channel ferryboats are superior to the Hovercrafts.

5. The first operating air-cushion vehicle was built by
    - a. a Finnish engineer.
    - b. an American inventor.
    - c. a German architect.

6. On the whole, the article tells about
    - a. a vehicle that travels on a cushion of air.
    - b. the time it takes to cross the English Channel.
    - c. vehicles that look like upside-down bathtubs.

7. Which statement does this article lead you to believe?
    - a. Hovercrafts may take the place of ferryboats someday.
    - b. The best way to cross a body of water is by ferry.
    - c. There are too many Hovercrafts in use in Finland.

8. Why was the first air-cushion vehicle not successful?
    - a. It did not use enough engine power.
    - b. Only Finnish people could use it.
    - c. It was impractical and uneconomical.

9. Think about the concept for this group of articles. Which statement seems true both for the article and for the concept?
    - a. A vehicle that travels on compressed air is not practical.
    - b. Many nations make plans for better means of transportation.
    - c. The English are the only people who plan better water travel.

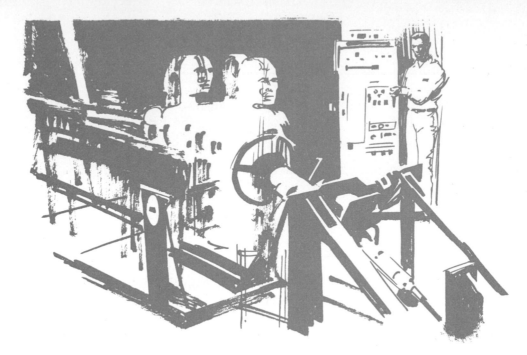

Planning for Safety

Between 1940 and 1967, the number of cars, trucks, and buses on American highways tripled. As roads became more crowded, auto accidents increased. By 1967, traffic accidents were causing 1,000 deaths a week. Every day 10,000 persons were injured.

As the toll climbed, many different groups were working to make highway travel safer. Highway planners designed safer roads, while educators tried to make more drivers safety-minded. Automotive engineers concentrated on making cars safer.

The engineers made a study of auto accidents. They learned that in many crashes, the passengers' bodies are thrown forward. The driver is likely to be thrown onto the steering column, which may go through the chest. Other passengers may strike the windshield, receiving head injuries or bad cuts if the glass breaks. When a car is struck from the rear, passengers' heads are snapped backwards often causing neck injuries.

As a result of this kind of study, all new cars, beginning with 1964 models, were equipped with seat belts. If properly fastened, the seat belts can prevent many injuries and reduce the severity of others. Congress passed laws requiring auto manufacturers to install other recommended safety devices.

A special worry is the number of injuries and deaths caused when cars strike fixed objects, like road signs. Although they can't remove many of the signs, safety experts are designing and testing devices to reduce injuries.

Some cities use barrels filled with sand to protect bridge ends or danger spots on busy roads. These are then bunched together in groups of five and six. If a car hits the barrels, the crash is absorbed in part by the sand. Baglike devices have been tried as well. These are filled with water. In a crash, the water softens the blow and helps reduce injuries.

1. Since 1964 all new cars have been equipped with
   a. headrests.   c. stronger sides.
   b. windshields.   d. seat belts.

2. The word in paragraph 5 that means *to lessen* is _____.

3. The words "like road signs" in paragraph 5 describe the _____.

4. While it is not directly stated, the article suggests that
   a. some accidents can be avoided.
   b. accidents are good for business.
   c. accidents are required by Congress.

5. The number of cars on our highways will continue to
   a. be baglike.
   b. increase.
   c. decrease.

6. On the whole, the article tells about
   a. traffic accidents in the year 1967.
   b. the different groups on highways.
   c. new safety devices.

7. Which statement does this article lead you to believe?
   a. The more crowded the roads are, the fewer accidents happen.
   b. Nobody cares when people are hurt or killed in accidents.
   c. Many different groups are concerned about traffic injuries.

8. Why are seat belts important when properly fastened?
   a. They prevent car doors from flying open during an accident.
   b. They prevent many injuries and reduce the severity of others.
   c. They keep passengers from leaving the scene of an accident.

9. Think about the concept for this group of articles. Which statement seems true both for the article and for the concept?
   a. The increase in travel makes better safety measures a necessity.
   b. In America accidents only happen on highways where tolls are paid.
   c. New cars should not be required to install any safety devices.

Nature Is Their Enemy

The National Gallery of Art in Washington, D.C., is one of the world's greatest art museums. Millions of persons have entered its doors to see paintings by the world's fine artists. But if these priceless masterpieces are to be preserved, the Gallery must protect them carefully. The Gallery's 135 guards have successfully prevented damage and theft, but protecting the paintings from nature is a greater problem.

In past times, the owners of paintings did not protect them from damaging changes in humidity and temperature. As a result, the life-spans of these paintings were shortened. In the National Gallery, however, humidity and temperature are carefully controlled. The building is air-conditioned in summer and heated in winter. The air-conditioning and heating systems are so important to the life of the paintings that the Gallery has two of each system. If one should fail, the extra one can take over.

Light is another enemy of paintings. Ultraviolet rays in light cause paintings to fade. Long ago, paintings often hung in dark churches and palaces. A coat of varnish was a protection from the weak light. But when museums took over the care of many paintings, they were often hung in brighter light than before. Soon they were in danger of fading. The damaging effects of light were increased when the museums removed the varnish coating, yellowed with age.

To protect its paintings, the National Gallery installed a special kind of glass in its skylights. This glass allows visible light to enter the building but it keeps out harmful ultraviolet rays. The Gallery has also developed new and better varnishes which help to keep paintings from fading. Thanks to these new precautions, many of the world's greatest paintings are being preserved for future generations to enjoy.

FIND THE ANSWERS

1. Ultraviolet rays in light cause paintings to
   - a. fade.
   - c. glare.
   - b. glow.
   - d. fall.

2. The word in the last paragraph that means *care taken ahead of time* is

   _____.

3. The words "in dark churches and palaces" in paragraph 3 tell about the

   _____.

4. While it is not directly stated, the article suggests that
   - a. great artists painted with coats of new varnish.
   - b. humidity and temperature cannot affect paintings.
   - c. some priceless paintings were not preserved.

5. The National Gallery of Art is in
   - a. Wappington, L.I.
   - b. Wilmington, N.C.
   - c. Washington, D.C.

6. On the whole, the article tells about
   - a. preserving millions of persons in buildings.
   - b. protecting great paintings from nature.
   - c. painting dark churches and palaces.

7. Which statement does this article lead you to believe?
   - a. Too much fuss is made about paintings that were done long ago.
   - b. The care of the world's greatest paintings is a big responsibility.
   - c. The National Gallery is the only museum that contains paintings.

8. Why did the museums remove varnish coatings from some paintings?
   - a. The coatings had yellowed with age.
   - b. They wanted the paintings to fade.
   - c. The coatings were beginning to peel.

9. Think about the concept for this group of articles. Which statement seems true both for the article and for the concept?
   - a. The National Gallery's 135 guards protect thieves.
   - b. Ultraviolet rays are permitted to enter the National Gallery.
   - c. Modern art galleries must plan their buildings carefully.

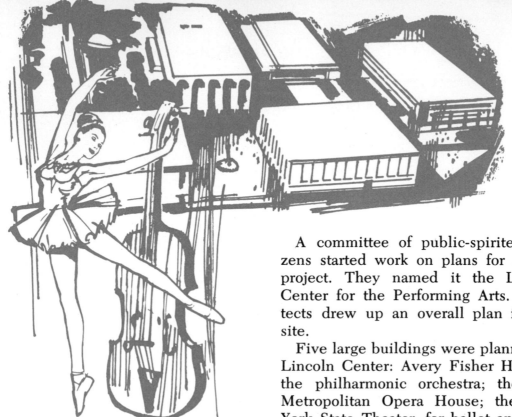

Putting the Arts Together

Three important things happened in 1955 in New York City. The Metropolitan Opera Association looked for a place to build a new opera house, since its old building was inadequate. The New York Philharmonic Orchestra was told that its old building would soon be torn down. Like the opera, the orchestra needed a new home. The city announced plans to clear a three-block slum area, as part of an urban renewal project.

To some people, the three things seemed to fit together. Why not build new homes, they asked, for both opera and orchestra, on the cleared slum site? Why not develop the area as a unified grouping of theaters and concert halls?

A committee of public-spirited citizens started work on plans for such a project. They named it the Lincoln Center for the Performing Arts. Architects drew up an overall plan for the site.

Five large buildings were planned for Lincoln Center: Avery Fisher Hall, for the philharmonic orchestra; the new Metropolitan Opera House; the New York State Theater, for ballet and light opera; the Vivian Beaumont Theater, for plays; and the Juilliard School where musicians, actors, and dancers would study. There would also be a library-museum, a bandshell for outdoor concerts, a fountain, and a reflecting pool.

Six different architectural firms were hired to design the buildings. They met together once a month, to make sure that each building would be in harmony with the overall plan.

Early in 1959, President Eisenhower broke ground for the first of the buildings. Ten years later, workers were completing the last of them. The dingy, rat-infested tenements were gone. In their places stood gleaming theaters and tree-shaded plazas. Today, all New York uses and enjoys its new and exciting Lincoln Center for education and entertainment.

1. The Lincoln Center is in
   a. New Haven.
   b. New York.
   c. the Metropolitan.
   d. New Mexico.

2. The word in paragraph 1 that means *having to do with the city* is

   _____ .

3. The words "of public-spirited citizens" in paragraph 3 describe a

   _____ .

4. While it is not directly stated, the article suggests that
   a. there are many slums in a big city.
   b. cities have very few slum areas.
   c. slum areas can never be cleared up.

5. The Juilliard School is for
   a. educators.
   b. musicians.
   c. opera.

6. On the whole, the article tells about
   a. the New York Philharmonic Orchestra.
   b. ground-breaking by President Eisenhower.
   c. an entertainment area that replaced a slum.

7. Which statement does this article lead you to believe?
   a. Entertainment at the Lincoln Center is quite varied.
   b. All you can see at the Lincoln Center is the ballet.
   c. A school does not belong at an entertainment center.

8. Why did six architectural firms meet once a month?
   a. They liked looking at themselves in the reflecting pool.
   b. They could not agree on the architecture of the buildings.
   c. They wanted to be sure all the buildings were in harmony.

9. Think about the concept for this group of articles. Which statement seems true both for the article and for the concept?
   a. Theaters and tree-shaded plazas cannot replace all tenements.
   b. A city can be made beautiful with the right planning.
   c. The people of New York City did not want the new center.

The Sword of Light

There once dwelt in Ireland a young lad named Patrick, who dearly loved to bet. He would bet how long it might take a cloud to pass overhead, or what color a stranger's eyes might be. In short, he would bet on anything.

One day Patrick was strolling on a path that meandered through a forest. As he walked, Patrick chanced to spy an old man in a dark glen, playing a solitary game of backgammon. Naturally, Patrick stopped to watch. After a while, he said courteously, "It's begging your pardon I am, sir, but are you betting your left hand against your right hand?"

"That's the way of it," the old man replied. "And it grieves me to think my right hand always wins, for I can only bet on my left hand." He glanced slyly up at Patrick. "Would you care to be making a small wager on one of my hands?"

"Since you're so obliging," Patrick answered, "I'll bet my last sixpence on the right hand."

"Done," the old man said, "and if you win I'll pay you a hundred guineas." He cleared his board and began a new game. In the twinkling of an eye, Patrick was richer by one hundred guineas.

"I'm thinking," Patrick mused to himself as he collected his winnings, "that the old man must be a sorcerer. But sure and that's no affair of mine." And off Patrick went to buy some acreage which he could farm. He worked hard at his farming, but in the back of his mind was the memory of the old man in the dark glen. Well, before you could spell *shillelagh*, Patrick was back in the glen betting again and winning. This time, instead of guineas, Patrick asked for the most beautiful girl in all of Ireland as his bride.

Next morning came a knocking at the farmhouse door, and when Patrick peered out, who should be standing there but the most beautiful girl in the world. "Who are you and how did you get here?" exclaimed Patrick.

"I was sent here by the old man in the glen," said the girl, smiling. "Am I not welcome then?"

"You are more than welcome," Patrick cried. The girl was happy to hear these words and consented to stay.

Sabina was the colleen's name. She and Patrick were married and lived well and happily together until Patrick again bethought himself of the old man in the glen.

"One last game," Patrick reflected, "to win garments of brocade for Sabina, some trinkets for her hair, and maybe an elegant shay to take her into town." That night, when Sabina was fast asleep, Patrick stole away to the glen.

"Have you come to bet on my right hand again?" the old man asked craftily.

"I have," said Patrick, "for Sabina needs garments of brocade, trinkets for her hair, and a shay to take her in style to town."

"She shall have them," said the old man, "if you win. However, should I win the game, I shall want you to fetch me the Sword of Light."

"Gladly," Patrick replied in his well-mannered way, "if you will tell me what it is and where to find it."

"It is far across the sea in a cavern well guarded by a fierce and vicious dragon," the old man answered. "It is sheathed in a dark scabbard and hidden deep inside the cavern. You shall fetch the sword for me, lad, or die trying."

"Only if I lose the game," Patrick reminded him. The old man grinned knowingly, for he had waited long and patiently for this moment.

"I seem to have lost," Patrick said later with great surprise when the game was over. "But surely you did not mean all that palaver about a Sword of Light."

"Mean it I did," the old man said grimly, "and fetch it for me you shall.

And until the Sword of Light is in my possession, you shall not close your eyes again, though you may perish for lack of sleep. One word of caution," the old man added as Patrick stumbled out of the glen. "Do not remove the Sword of Light from its sheath. You must hand the sword to me in its scabbard."

Poor Patrick went home and tried to sleep, but it was as the old man had predicted. Try as he would, Patrick could not close his weary eyes. At last he woke Sabina and told her his sorry tale.

"I am the old man's niece," Sabina said then, "and I can do a little magic of my own. I will help you on one condition, but you must promise me faithfully that you will never bet on anything again." As soon as Patrick promised, Sabina gave him an enchanted horse and a magic harp. She placed her hands lightly over Patrick's ears, saying, "The harp shall play of its own accord, but you shall not hear its melody."

Patrick mounted the magic steed at once and flew off over land and sea to the cavern guarded by the monstrous dragon. As soon as Patrick reached the cave, the harp filled the air with music. Its melody was so haunting and strange that the birds fell silent, and the summer breezes stopped blowing. The dragon wept bitter tears and let Patrick pass without so much as a sideward glance. Quickly Patrick located the Sword of Light, seized it in its scabbard, and remounted his horse. Back he flew to the glen, where the old man was still playing his game of backgammon.

"Now perhaps I can sleep again," the weary Patrick cried, and he began to pull the Sword of Light from its sheath.

"Do not unsheath it, wretched lad!"

the old man shouted in fury. But it was too late, for Patrick had already freed the sword from its scabbard. A blinding light spread throughout the glen. "You have destroyed me," the old man wailed, and he disappeared in a flurry of smoke.

As for Patrick, he rushed home where he fell into a deep sleep that lasted for two days and two nights. When he finally awoke, the new Patrick never bet on anything again.

The Sword of Light, some say, is still there, deep in the woods, filling the glen with a wondrous light, as if the morning sun rises from that very spot. And should you by chance stumble into the light someday, you will see and hear magic no other mortal has ever known.

1087 words

IV

Where Might Change Take Us?

In this section you will read some of the predictions about how life tomorrow may be lived. You will read about these things in the areas of history, space, biology, anthropology, economics, geography, earth science, mathematics, engineering, and art.

Keep these questions in mind when you are reading.

1. What are some recent changes that may affect all our lives?

2. What things may happen because of recent changes?

3. How will we change as individuals because of things that may happen?

4. What kinds of change would you like to see now?

5. What part could you play in making changes?

One Man's Peaceful War

In the 1950s the Italian architect Danilo Dolci visited western Sicily. It was, he said, "the most wretched piece of country I had ever seen." A long history of ignorance and poverty overshadowed the area, which is part of an island off the Italian coast.

In some villages, the people burned manure rather than spread it on their fields to enrich the soil. They did not understand erosion. They thought that magic spells caused the soil to disappear from their hillside farms. Few people could read and write. Few children went to school. There was almost no industry. Not able to make a living, many people had turned to crime. Some of the politicians who governed the area were themselves criminals who benefited by keeping the people poor and ignorant.

Danilo Dolci gave up a promising career and began to devote his life to helping the Sicilians. He taught them to plan peaceful demonstrations that would call the Italian government's attention to their problems. Under Dolci's direction, some Sicilians staged a "strike in reverse" by repairing roads—without pay. Dolci advised the people to ask the government for jobs rather than money, for irrigation dams, and for agricultural experts to teach them better ways to farm.

Finally, some constructive help came from the Italian government, and living conditions in Sicily are slowly improving.

Danilo Dolci believes that in backward areas, the people themselves must work to better their conditions. But in some parts of the world, people are too uneducated to know what they need or how to go about asking for it.

Needed in the future will be more far-seeing leaders like Dolci, to go into backward nations and help bring about peaceful change. Such leaders will be the heroes of tomorrow's history books.

FIND THE ANSWERS

1. In some villages in western Sicily, the people did not understand
   - a. erosion.
   - b. poverty.
   - c. animals.
   - d. industry.

2. The word in paragraph 1 that means *state of knowing little or nothing* is

   _____ .

3. The words "who governed the area were themselves criminals" in paragraph 2

   describe some of the _____ .

4. While it is not directly stated, the article suggests that
   - a. ignorant people make the best farmers.
   - b. magicians make trouble for farmers.
   - c. people need to know more about the land.

5. Danilo Dolci gave up a promising career as
   - a. an engineer.
   - b. an architect.
   - c. a politician.

6. On the whole, the article tells about
   - a. one individual's fight to help a group of people.
   - b. large secret groups of troublemakers.
   - c. villagers who work on farms without pay.

7. Which statement does this article lead you to believe?
   - a. One person can never hope to bring about any changes.
   - b. Good planning can help a country progress and grow.
   - c. Ignorance, poverty, and crime make a country strong.

8. What happened as a result of Dolci's actions?
   - a. Living conditions in Sicily are improving.
   - b. All strikes in Sicily are held backwards.
   - c. Magicians in Sicily became agricultural experts.

9. Think about the concept for this group of articles. Which statement seems true both for the article and for the concept?
   - a. Individuals may make important contributions to their country.
   - b. Individuals should not try to understand their country's problems.
   - c. Few individuals can really contribute to their country.

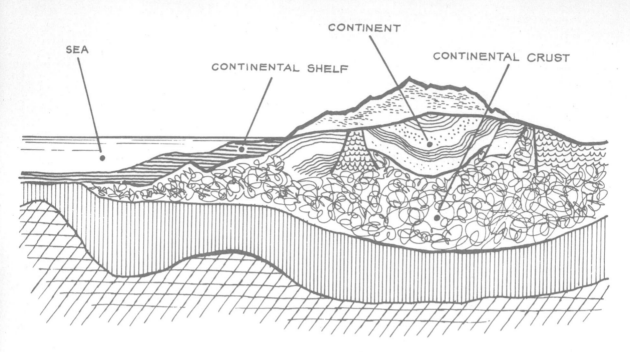

Labels on diagram: SEA, CONTINENTAL SHELF, CONTINENT, CONTINENTAL CRUST

New Frontier Underwater

Throughout history, many nations have gained land by fighting wars or by sending explorers to plant their nation's flag in newly discovered lands. The strongest nations or the nations with the most daring explorers usually took possession of new frontiers with all their valuable resources.

One of today's new frontiers is the ocean floor. Oil and natural gas are already being pumped from undersea wells. Undersea springs may provide new supplies of fresh water. Undersea farms may grow fish and plants for use as valuable minerals. But who owns the ocean floor?

In 1959, eighty-six nations agreed to a treaty which stated that nations own underwater land off their coasts to a depth of 656 feet, but added "or to the depth they are technically able to explore." This means that only coastal nations own the rich, easy-to-explore continental shelves. It also means that the nations with the best diving equipment can explore and claim the deeper parts of the sea.

Today, landlocked nations are asking that some of the undersea frontier be saved for them. They feel it would not be fair to let the coastal nations have the continental shelves. It would not be fair, say some nations, to let the nations with the best underwater exploring equipment claim the most underwater land. There would be nothing left for landlocked nations but the deepest, poorest parts of the sea.

In the future, undersea land beyond a very narrow limit may be controlled by a branch of the United Nations. Nations will be allowed to develop some parts for peaceful purposes. Most of the ocean floor will belong to everyone, and the riches of the new frontier will benefit all the nations of the world.

FIND THE ANSWERS

1. Undersea wells are being pumped for oil and
   a. salt.
   b. minerals.
   c. food plants.
   d. natural gas.

2. The word in paragraph 5 that means *serve* or *bring good to* is

   _____ .

3. The words "beyond a very narrow limit" in paragraph 5 refer to

   _____ _____ .

4. While it is not directly stated, the article suggests that
   a. most nations have sea coasts of their own.
   b. the ocean floor is one of our last frontiers.
   c. nothing valuable can be found on the ocean floor.

5. Throughout history, nations often gained land by
   a. exploring the ocean floor.
   b. fighting wars.
   c. mining the sea.

6. On the whole, the article tells about
   a. rich and easy-to-explore continental shelves.
   b. valuable undersea land and who shall own it.
   c. daring explorers who own the ocean floor.

7. Which statement does this article lead you to believe?
   a. In earlier days, nations might have gone to war over undersea land.
   b. All valuable resources on land have been used up.
   c. Nations today no longer want to own their own resources.

8. Why are landlocked nations claiming that other nations are unfair?
   a. The other nations won't let the landlocked nations move to the sea.
   b. The landlocked nations are being forced to sell their underwater equipment.
   c. Other nations have left them only the deepest, poorest parts of the sea.

9. Think about the concept for this group of articles. Which statement seems true both for the article and for the concept?
   a. The only food that anyone can expect to get from the sea is fish.
   b. Someday, undersea land may produce great benefits to all men.
   c. No one will want to eat food from undersea farms.

An Observatory on the Moon

A scientist once said that studying the stars from the earth is something like looking up at the sky from the bottom of a swimming pool. Even on the clearest night the earth's dense atmosphere screens out 30 percent of the light from any star. Air turbulence causes stars to twinkle. Through a telescope, the stars seem to jump around dizzily.

Because the moon has no atmosphere, astronomers are looking forward to setting up an observatory there. On the moon, there will be no clouds to obscure the view. The sky will appear dark at all times, so astronomers can work twenty-four hours a day. Because there is no air turbulence, the stars will appear steady through a telescope.

Because the moon is relatively near the earth, moon-based astronomers will see the stars in the familiar patterns known on earth. They will not need new star maps of the sky. Stars seen from the moon will appear to move very slowly. Because the earth rotates on its axis once every twenty-four hours, earth-based astronomers see the stars hurry across the sky each night. The moon rotates on its axis only once a month. To astronomers on the moon, the stars will appear to stand almost still. Moon-based astronomers will have much more time to focus their telescopes and take time-exposure photographs.

On the earth, mechanical radio noises jam the airwaves and interfere with the reception of radio signals from certain stars. A radio telescope located on the far side of the moon will be permanently protected from such interference.

It won't be easy to put telescopes on the moon. However, astronomers are certain the job can be done. They are convinced that the moon is an ideal place to set up an observatory.

1. The moon rotates on its axis once every
    a. twenty-four hours.   c. night.
    b. month.   d. twenty minutes.

2. The word in paragraph 1 that means *thick* or *solid* is _____ .

3. The words "in the familiar patterns known on earth" in paragraph 3 refer to the _____ .

4. While it is not directly stated, the article suggests that
    a. there are always clouds around stars and planets.
    b. we still do not know very much about the stars.
    c. the stars are too dizzy to study.

5. Stars twinkle because of
    a. air turbulence.
    b. radio signals.
    c. light screens.

6. On the whole, the article tells about
    a. the far side of the moon and stars.
    b. taking time-exposure photographs.
    c. studying the stars from a moon base.

7. Which statement does the article lead you to believe?
    a. Astronomers want the stars to remain the same so the maps won't change.
    b. People now know everything to be known about the earth.
    c. Research in space may teach us more than we can now imagine.

8. Why do astronomers look forward to setting up an observatory on the moon?
    a. The moon has airwaves that jam.
    b. The moon has no atmosphere.
    c. The moon hurries across the sky.

9. Think about the concept for this group of articles. Which statement seems true both for the article and for the concept?
    a. Moon astronomers will come to earth to work.
    b. People from earth cannot live on the moon.
    c. Someday people may live and work on the moon.

the nearest star. The power and burning time of a chemical rocket engine is too limited. It is not practical to build one capable of carrying the huge load of fuel and oxidizer that would be needed for a long trip into outer space.

For a deep space mission, a rocket engine would have to operate much longer and produce much more power than the present engines. The nuclear rocket engines being tested will serve better than the chemical rocket engines. They produce more power from each pound of fuel than chemical engines and they will operate longer. But space scientists are thinking even farther ahead. They are planning new rocket engines that will use unusual forms of power such as light energy.

A beam of light is a stream of fast-moving particles called photons. As they move at a speed of 186,000 miles per second, the photons exert a very slight pressure. It is this photon pressure in sunlight that forces the tails of comets to stream away from the sun.

If a rocket engine could produce a stream of photons with enough power, it might propel a spacecraft. Instead of the combustion chamber, nozzle, and fuel tank of today's rocket engine, the photon rocket engine would have a giant saucer-shaped mirror. The mirror would collect light and reflect it in a focused beam. As the great heat produced would melt any material known today, the mirror would have to be made of some new material.

Space scientists are not yet ready to build a photon rocket engine. But they can guess at how it might look. It could resemble a flashlight flying backward on its own beam of light.

Tomorrow:

The Flying Flashlight

Rocket engines that burn chemical fuel have carried astronauts to the moon. But such engines will not carry them to

1. Scientists are planning new rocket engines that might use
      a. chemical fuel.   c. nuclear energy.
      b. light energy.   d. nozzles and tanks.

2. The word in paragraph 2 that means *a project or task* is _____.

3. The words "flying backward on its own beam of light" in paragraph 5 describe

   a _____ .

4. While it is not directly stated, the article suggests that
      a. there are several unusual forms of energy.
      b. there is only one form of energy to use.
      c. scientists know nothing about the use of energy.

5. A beam of light is a stream of fast-moving particles called
      a. phases.
      b. photons.
      c. comets.

6. On the whole, the article tells about
      a. rocket engines that burn too much chemical fuel.
      b. a rocket engine made up of flying flashlights.
      c. using an unusual form of energy to travel in space.

7. Which statement does this article lead you to believe?
      a. Scientists only want to perfect the engines they have now.
      b. Scientists have no real hope of ever building a photon rocket.
      c. Scientists may even improve on a photon rocket engine someday.

8. Why would the mirror have to be made of some new material?
      a. The great heat will produce chemicals dangerous for the engine.
      b. The materials of today will be used up by the time the new engine is ready.
      c. The great heat produced would melt any material known today.

9. Think about the concept for this group of articles. Which statement seems true both for the article and for the concept?
      a. People hope to reach the stars one day.
      b. People have begun to reach their limits.
      c. The stars are already too close to us.

New Medicines from the Sea

The earth's oceans, which cover 70 percent of the earth's surface, are a frontier that we are just beginning to explore. Scientists know that the undersea world is a storehouse of oil, minerals, and protein-rich foods. The oceans are also a storehouse of plants and animals. Some of these living things contain substances that can be made into useful medicines.

Scientists have long known that seawater speeds the healing of certain kinds of wounds. Medical experts believe that certain fungi floating in seawater may be responsible. One new medicine, cephalothin (sə fal′ə thən) is already being made from a fungus that floats in the Mediterranean Sea. Cephalothin kills certain germs that penicillin will not kill.

The fungus used to make cephalothin is only one of about 300 kinds of fungi in the sea. Many of these fungi have not yet been studied. Some may yield even more valuable medicines than cephalothin.

Anyone who has ever stepped on the jellyfish called the Portuguese man-of-war knows that it contains a powerful, stinging poison. Medical researchers have studied this poison. They have also studied the poisons of sea snakes, octopuses, shell animals, and sponges. In very small quantities, some of these poisons have proved useful in the treatment of diabetes, heart disease, ulcers, and spastic paralysis.

So far, only about one percent of all the sea's forms of animal life have been studied. The time required to col-

lect any one form of sea life in large quantities has held back research.

Before too many years, however, scientists will be able to work under the sea for long periods of time. They will live in structures like the Sealabs. Among these scientists will be doctors testing sea life for new and better kinds of medicines.

154

1. Cephalothin comes from a
   a. plant.
   c. fungus.
   b. sponge.
   d. fish.

2. The word in sentence 6 that means *a group of lower plants that includes molds* is _____ .

3. The words "which cover 70 percent of the earth's surface" in paragraph 1 describe the earth's _____ .

4. While it is not directly stated, the article suggests that
   a. it is good for a diabetic to be stung by a jellyfish.
   b. scientists have always experimented with poisons.
   c. new attitudes about poisonous substances are developing.

5. Cephalothin comes from one of
   a. the jellyfish family.
   b. 300 kinds of fungi.
   c. 800 kinds of fungi.

6. On the whole, this article tells about
   a. the sea as a source of new medicines.
   b. using seawater to treat heart disease.
   c. stepping on fish that can sting you.

7. Which statement does this article lead you to believe?
   a. Serious exploration of the ocean is already under way.
   b. There are no frontiers left to explore.
   c. The ocean will not be explored in the near future.

8. What will make it possible for scientists to be able to work under the sea?
   a. People are learning to breathe under water for longer periods.
   b. Doctors will live in Portuguese submarines.
   c. They will live in structures like the Sealabs.

9. Think about the concept for this group of articles. Which statement seems true both for the article and for the concept?
   a. All our diseases will be conquered by medicines from the sea.
   b. Some diseases may disappear with the help of new sea medicines.
   c. Some diseases can never be treated by any of our doctors.

THE AMERICAN ELM

New Trees to Resist Disease

The American elm tree, with its gracefully arching branches, was once a common sight throughout the eastern half of the United States. In 1930, however, some elm logs were imported from the Netherlands. These logs contained beetles and a deadly fungus. The beetles spread the fungi to living American elm trees. By 1969 most American elms were dead or dying.

In the future a new kind of elm may replace the dying trees. The new elm will be just as beautiful as the American elm but it will be resistant to the Dutch elm disease.

In the past, attempts to crossbreed the American elm with other kinds of elms that are disease resistant, have all failed. At last, scientists know why they failed. Today they think they know what to do about it.

The American elm's pollen cells contain twice as many chromosomes as the pollen cells of other elms. If their chromosome numbers differ, plants cannot be crossbred.

Now scientists have discovered that a chemical called colchicine (käl′chə sēn′) will double the chromosomes in plant cells. At research centers, pollen cells of seedling Siberian elms are being treated with colchicine. These trees are developing the same number of chromosomes as the American elm. When the new Siberian elms are mature they will be crossbred with American elms. It is hoped that the result will be a new kind of elm. The new tree will look like the American elm but will have the Siberian elm's resistance to Dutch elm disease.

Using colchicine, plant breeders have already crossbred wheat and rye. The high-yielding grain that resulted from the new plant is called triticale (trit′ ə kā′ lē). If the new elm tree is as successful as the new plant that produced triticale, scientists may use colchicine to create more new and useful plants for the future.

1. In 1930, some elm logs were imported from the
    a. Navassa Islands.
    c. New Hebrides.
    b. Netherlands.
    d. Philippines.

2. The word in paragraph 4 that means *threadlike bodies in the nucleus of a cell* is _____ .

3. The words "with its gracefully arching branches" in paragraph 1 refer to the American _____ _____ .

4. While it is not directly stated, the article suggests that
    a. the country paid a high price for importing infected logs.
    b. not too much is known about plants.
    c. the Siberian elm is the most disease-resistant plant that grows.

5. The seedling Siberian elms are being treated with
    a. chromosomes.
    b. triticale.
    c. colchicine.

6. On the whole, the article tells about
    a. the number of chromosomes in wheat and rye plants.
    b. a log scientists tried to crossbreed with an elm.
    c. crossbreeding plants to create stronger strains.

7. Which statement does this article lead you to believe?
    a. Americans loved their elm trees very much.
    b. The American elm was killed off by Dutch spies.
    c. We don't need elm trees in this country.

8. Why did scientists choose Siberian elms for their research?
    a. They are resistant to the Dutch elm disease.
    b. They contain more colchicine than the American elm trees.
    c. They have more chromosomes than the American elm tree.

9. Think about the concept for this group of articles. Which statement seems true both for the article and for the concept?
    a. It is not important to us if plants begin to die out.
    b. Plants of the future may be superior to plants we have now.
    c. Scientists try to improve on nature to prove how clever they are.

Faraway Places Just Like Home

In the past, foreign travel has been costly and time-consuming. Until the jet age, it was generally only the well-to-do or the very adventurous persons who visited the faraway places of the world.

Soon the giant supersonic airplanes now being built and tested will make foreign travel faster and less costly. As a result, Europeans may casually plan weekend visits to San Francisco or Tokyo. Americans may weekend in Turkey or Tahiti. One travel expert believes that the average American will visit Europe at least fifteen times in his lifetime.

But when tomorrow's travelers reach faraway places, they'll find them more alike than they are today. It's possible that people all over the world will be eating some of the same kinds of food. They may also be wearing very similar clothing.

Cultural differences between peoples will become less marked. Regional language differences and quaint provincial customs will tend to vanish, except where they are intentionally preserved by people proud of their cultural heritage.

Some experts believe that the world of the future will be bilingual or trilingual. They believe that there will be two or three international languages in use. Other experts believe that one language alone will become dominant everywhere for use in all international communications. The single international language might well be that of the first nation to begin full-time, world-wide television broadcasting relayed by a chain of orbiting communication satellites.

Television and supersonic transportation will make the world seem smaller. They will bring far-apart peoples closer together. They will also tend to make different peoples more alike. There will be more foreign travel, but the travelers of the future may find foreign lands much less foreign.

FIND THE ANSWERS

1. Americans may someday weekend in
   - a. San Francisco or Tokyo.   c. Turkey or Tahiti.
   - b. Taiwan and Tennessee.   d. Thailand or Texas.

2. The word in paragraph 5 that means *able to speak two languages* is

   _____ .

3. The words "proud of their cultural heritage" in paragraph 4 describe

   _____ .

4. While it is not directly stated, the article suggests that
   - a. experts predict that all Europeans will lose their customs.
   - b. most people want to travel to foreign lands.
   - c. Americans are the only people who travel much.

5. Quaint provincial customs will tend to
   - a. improve.
   - b. appear.
   - c. vanish.

6. On the whole, the article tells about
   - a. Europeans who plan their weekend visits around the world.
   - b. the kind of food and clothing people will have someday.
   - c. the loss of cultural and language differences in the future.

7. Which statement does this article lead you to believe?
   - a. Most people will be unable to speak a foreign language.
   - b. People will be better able to communicate with each other.
   - c. There will be many more languages in the world of tomorrow.

8. Why will the world seem smaller?
   - a. Television and supersonic transportation will bring distant peoples together.
   - b. The world will begin to shrink when far-apart peoples live closer.
   - c. Orbiting communication satellites will force languages to die.

9. Think about the concept for this group of articles. Which statement seems true both for the article and for the concept?
   - a. International communications requires a single language.
   - b. People of the future will find it easier to understand each other.
   - c. Americans will never learn a second language.

Taller or Smaller?

We have learned a great deal about how physical traits are passed from generation to generation. Scientists know that DNA molecules in human cells carry inherited physical traits in a sort of chemical code.

Someday we may learn how to change these DNA molecules so as to change the physical traits they carry. Eventually, parents may be able to choose what traits their children will inherit: blue eyes or brown, tall bodies or short.

Most children of today are taller than their parents, but this may be due to better nutrition rather than to an inherited change. In some population groups, height is increasing one inch per generation.

Is it a good thing for people to get taller and taller? No, say certain experts. The human skeleton would be strained carrying the weight of a very tall body. In a world where workers use power tools for heavy work, there is no special advantage in great height or strength. It might be better, some say, if people got smaller.

Smaller humans would need less food and could live in smaller houses. They would fit more comfortably into cramped spacecraft. They would drive smaller cars on narrower roads. Smaller people would make the world seem larger and less crowded. The world's natural resources would last longer. So it is possible that if scientists learn to control inherited physical traits, they might speak out for a reduction in human size.

Anthropologists have estimated the heights of ancient peoples from fossil bones. They have compared these

heights with the heights of people now living in all parts of the world. The evidence appears that most people are getting taller. The human of tomorrow may be still taller—unless he or she decides to be smaller.

1. One reason children today are taller than their parents may be because of better
       a. nutrition.   c. ancestors.
       b. DNA.   d. anthropologists.

2. The word in paragraph 1 that means *certain qualities or features* is

   _____ .

3. The words "carrying the weight of a very tall body" in paragraph 4 refer to the

   human _____ .

4. While it is not directly stated, the article suggests that
       a. tall people must drive smaller cars.
       b. it is always better to be taller.
       c. there are advantages to being small.

5. Someday scientists may learn how to change
       a. DNA molecules.
       b. fossil bones.
       c. nutrition.

6. On the whole, the article tells about
       a. human strength needed for heavy work.
       b. human height today and in the future.
       c. anthropologists who study fossil bones.

7. Which statement does this article lead you to believe?
       a. Scientists want to keep people small so they can be controlled.
       b. Scientists think humans of the future should all be very tall.
       c. Scientists may control the size of humans of the future.

8. Why are scientists able to tell the height of ancient peoples?
       a. They can tell by looking at their pictures.
       b. They can estimate the heights from fossil bones.
       c. They know all old people must be quite small.

9. Think about the concept for this group of articles. Which statement seems true both for the article and for the concept?
       a. Humans of the future may be a product of their own planning.
       b. It is against the law to try to change your physical traits.
       c. Humans of the future will be the tallest ever to live.

Electronic Money

Before many years pass, a person may earn money and then spend it without handling coins, bills, or even checks. He or she may carry an all-purpose identification card.

Bankers guess that cash and checks will become rare as bank computers take over more of our bookkeeping and bill-paying. Eventually, a nationwide network of computers may handle almost all financial transactions. Homes and business places may be tied into this computer network just as they are now tied into telephone service.

The new system may work something like this for Barb Green, a woman of the future. At regular intervals, a computer at Barb's bank would transfer a credit representing Barb's salary from her employer's account to Barb's account. Then the computer would transfer smaller credits to other accounts for fixed bills like rent and car payments. These transactions would be arranged in advance and programmed into the bank's computer.

When Barb decides she can afford new clothes, she shows her identification card to a store clerk. The salesperson uses a push-button telephone to contact the bank computer. The computer transfers credit from Barb's bank account to the store's account. Barb's new clothes are paid for immediately.

Each transfer of money would take place instantly. There would be no waiting for monthly bank statements or payment checks to travel through the mail. There would be little chance for error, since all details of Barb's financial transactions would be stored in the computer's memory.

If the computer takes over, it may be possible to get along without money. But most banks think that Barb Green will still need to carry a little cash. Suppose she wants to buy a sack of peanuts or pay a bus fare. Then, a coin may be better than an all-purpose identification card.

FIND THE ANSWERS

1. Each transfer of money would take place
   - a. instantly.
   - b. regularly.
   - c. by television.
   - d. by cash.

2. The word in paragraph 2 that means *at a later time* is

   _____ .

3. The words "a woman of the future" in paragraph 3 describe _____

   _____ .

4. While it is not directly stated, the article suggests that
   - a. Barb Green will be the world's best bookkeeper.
   - b. it is always better to buy on credit.
   - c. computers make fewer mistakes than people.

5. Financial transactions would be stored in the
   - a. push-button telephone.
   - b. bank's new vaults.
   - c. computer's memory.

6. On the whole, the article tells about
   - a. handling coins, bills, and even checks.
   - b. financial transactions in the future.
   - c. a woman who has an identification card.

7. Which statement does this article lead you to believe?
   - a. People of the future will never have bills to pay.
   - b. People will not get into debt as easily as they do now.
   - c. Stores of the future will have to wait a long time to be paid.

8. Why will Barb Green carry a little cash?
   - a. She may need coins for small purchases.
   - b. She may think it is good luck to carry it.
   - c. She may want to feel it in her pocket.

9. Think about the concept for this group of articles. Which statement seems true both for the article and for the concept?
   - a. People will never again have to pay for things they buy.
   - b. The credit system of the future will be very different from the one now.
   - c. People of the future will not receive salaries for their work.

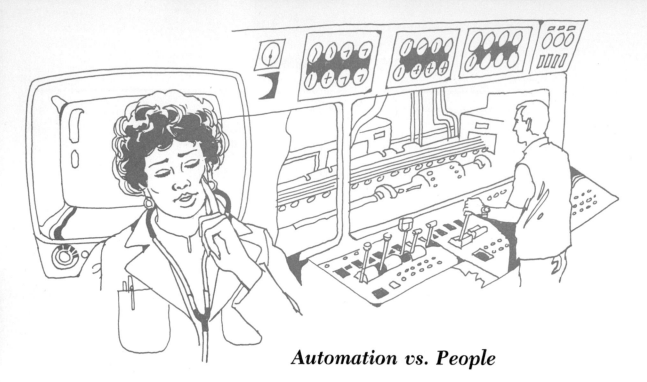

Automation vs. People

In factories and stores, in offices and on farms, new machines are taking over many jobs that used to be done by people. Today, one person operates a small factory from a single control panel. One computer takes over the tasks of dozens of office workers, while vending machines replace salesclerks in stores.

In the future, machines will continue to do even more of the world's work. Some people fear that there will not be enough work left for people to do in an age of automation. Surprisingly, however, the new machines often create new jobs. Engineers will be needed to design even better machines, while skilled technicians will be needed to install them, keep them operating, and repair them.

Fortunately, there will always be some jobs that machines cannot do. Many of these jobs have to do with helping other people.

No machine will replace doctors, nurses, and the others who help them care for sick people, for babies, and for the very old. No machine will replace the social worker or counselor who helps people in trouble. Teaching machines and television will be useful tools in the classroom, but they will not replace teachers. Machines are not likely to replace lawyers, ministers, police officers, firefighters, or day-care workers.

As newer and better machines are built, work patterns will have to change. Employees will keep going back to school to learn new skills, and this will create jobs for more teachers.

New and better machines will save time so that employees will work shorter hours. Most people will have more leisure time. This will create new jobs in businesses connected with hobbies, entertainment, and sports.

Increasing automation will create some unemployment, but it will also create new opportunities. No matter how many machines are invented, there will still be work for people to do.

1. Salesclerks in stores may be replaced by
    a. control panels.   c. technicians.
    b. vending machines.   d. supervisors.

2. The word in paragraph 2 that means *mechanical systems for doing work* is

    _____.

3. The words "that used to be done by people" in paragraph 1 refer to

    _____.

4. While it is not directly stated, the article suggests that
    a. people want doctors to be teaching machines.
    b. people are still more important than machines.
    c. people should be replaced by better machines.

5. As new and better machines are built, work patterns will
    a. have to change.
    b. stay the same.
    c. become less skilled.

6. On the whole, the article tells about
    a. sick people and old persons who are machines.
    b. replacing all people with much better machines.
    c. people and machines in the age of automation.

7. Which statement does this article lead you to believe?
    a. Machines will soon do all the teaching needed.
    b. No one will ever need to go to school again.
    c. Education will always be important.

8. Why will people have more leisure time?
    a. They will all be unemployed.
    b. They will work shorter hours.
    c. Machines will do all the work.

9. Think about the concept for this group of articles. Which statement seems true both for the article and for the concept?
    a. People may need skills we know nothing about in today's world.
    b. The skills people have will always be exactly as they are right now.
    c. In the future, skilled technicians will have the only good jobs.

Pavements for Tomorrow's Farms

In farming areas where the soil is sandy, rainfall quickly disappears. The moisture seeps down through the soil. As a result, the top layers of soil are almost as dry as they were before the rain. It is in the top layers of soil that the roots of young plants grow.

Asphalt paving like that used on many of today's roads may someday increase the crop yield of sandy farmland in many parts of the world. A thin layer of asphalt can help to hold moisture where plant roots can use it.

In the future, farms in sandy areas may have a waterproof asphalt floor under their sandy fields. New machines will lift a two-foot-thick layer of topsoil. The machines will then spray a thin layer of hot asphalt underneath. Finally, the machines will drop the topsoil back into place. When the asphalt hardens, it will trap moisture and keep it within reach of plant roots. Where this method

was tested in Michigan, potatoes were planted over asphalt. The potatoes that resulted were three times as large and heavy as potatoes growing in an untreated field nearby.

Another approach may be to spray a thin film of a black liquid, made from petroleum, on top of the soil after seeds are planted. The thin film prevents the loss of precious moisture by evaporation. The black surface also warms the soil underneath by absorbing heat from the sun rather than reflecting heat as a light-colored material would. The covered seeds sprout sooner and grow faster. The young plants easily push through the thin film.

Used on the surface of a field, such a black liquid can increase crop yields by 59 to 90 percent. It may prove most useful in Northern Europe, where the growing season is short, and in semi-desert areas of Asia and Latin America.

FIND THE ANSWERS

1. The black liquid can increase crop yields by
   - a. 59 to 90 percent.
   - b. three times.
   - c. 15 to 34 percent.
   - d. 99 percent.

2. The word in paragraph 1 that means *drains through a substance* is

   _____ .

3. The words "like that used on many of today's roads" in paragraph 2 describe

   _____ _____ .

4. While it is not directly stated, the article suggests that
   - a. the growing season is short in Northern Europe.
   - b. large crop yields are important only in Michigan.
   - c. it is important to increase crop yields around the world.

5. The black liquid that might be sprayed on top of the soil would be made from
   - a. asphalt.
   - b. petroleum.
   - c. topsoil.

6. On the whole, the article tells about
   - a. the kind of paving used on today's roads.
   - b. methods to trap moisture in topsoil for plants.
   - c. light-colored materials that reflect heat.

7. Which statement does this article lead you to believe?
   - a. Only oil can hold moisture where plant roots can get it.
   - b. Farming ideas are being shared around the world.
   - c. Farmers who have land in sandy areas have never grown crops.

8. Why is it a good idea to spray a film on the top of soil?
   - a. The film helps the moisture to evaporate more quickly.
   - b. The film helps the farmer see where to plant seeds.
   - c. The film prevents loss of moisture by evaporation.

9. Think about the concept for this group of articles. Which statement seems true both for the article and for the concept?
   - a. Someday there will be no deserts anywhere.
   - b. Asia and Latin America do not need good crop yields.
   - c. Deserts could yield fruitful crops someday.

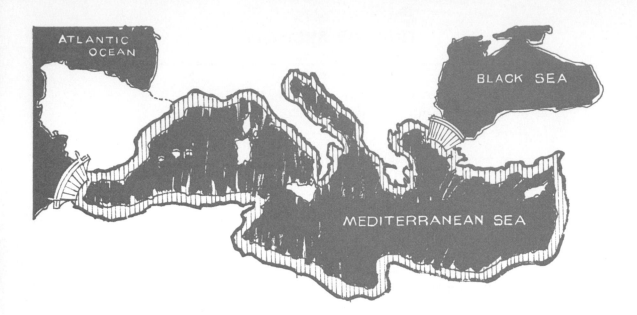

Changing a Sea into a Lake

The Mediterranean Sea was once a pair of lakes. One of the lakes was east of Italy's boot-shaped peninsula. The other was west of it. When the Ice Age ended and the continental glaciers melted, the level of the world's oceans rose. Water from the Atlantic flowed into the lakes. Many square miles of fertile land bordering the lakes disappeared underwater.

By building a dam across the Strait of Gibralter and lowering the level of the Mediterranean, people may win back this land someday. Once the Strait of Gibralter is closed off, evaporation from the surface of the Mediterranean would lower the water level by 20 to 40 inches a year. New land would appear all around the edge of the Mediterranean. The new land could provide croplands and additional living space for the crowded populations of the future.

The countries that border the Mediterranean would gain about 100,000 square miles of fertile land. Maps of Europe, Asia, and Africa would all look very different. The Mediterranean Sea would be a lake.

The project is not likely to be undertaken in the near future. Damming the Strait of Gibralter would be enormously difficult. The dam would have to be 18 miles long. It would also have to be tall and extremely strong to withstand immense pressure from the sea. The dam would have to be by-passed by a ship canal with locks. A smaller dam would be needed across the Dardanelles, east of Greece, in order to seal the Black Sea off from the Mediterranean.

Turning the Mediterranean Sea into a shrinking lake would require the close cooperation of the many different nations who would be losing their fine harbors on that body of water. They would pay with their harbors for the benefit of new farmland and living space.

1. The Mediterranean Sea was once a
    - a. pair of lakes.
    - b. shrinking lake.
    - c. glacial lake.
    - d. Greek lake.

2. The word in paragraph 1 that means *a stretch of land with water around three sides* is _____ .

3. The words "across the Dardanelles, east of Greece" in paragraph 4 describe a _____ .

4. While it is not directly stated, the article suggests that
    - a. the surface of the earth keeps changing.
    - b. our earth has always looked as it does now.
    - c. only people can change the surface of the earth.

5. A dam across the Strait of Gibraltar would have to be
    - a. 18 miles long.
    - b. 100,000 miles long.
    - c. smaller than the dam to seal off the Black Sea.

6. On the whole, the article tells about
    - a. the crowded populations of Asia in the future.
    - b. reclaiming land from the Mediterranean Sea.
    - c. the origin of the Mediterranean and the Black Sea.

7. Which statement does this article lead you to believe?
    - a. It is not difficult to find ways to gain more land.
    - b. People are looking for ways to find more land.
    - c. There is enough land on earth now to serve the future.

8. Why would different nations benefit even if they lost their fine harbors?
    - a. They would gain small dams with great pressures.
    - b. They would gain ship canals with many locks.
    - c. They would gain farmland and living space.

9. Think about the concept for this group of articles. Which statement seems true both for the article and for the concept?
    - a. Someday all the maps of the world will have to be changed.
    - b. Someday all the seas will turn into evaporated surfaces.
    - c. Someday people may be in need of more living space.

Steam to Save a Valley

In the Western United States, Mexico, Italy, Iceland, and New Zealand are huge underground reservoirs of very hot water. Some of the water is impure, having absorbed salt and other minerals from the earth. The water has been heated by contact with molten rock thrust up near the earth's surface by volcanic action. When a well is drilled into the water pocket, a jet of steam shoots high into the air.

One enormous hot-water pocket lies under the fertile but dry Imperial Valley of Southern California. This reservoir may someday be tapped to solve two of the area's problems: a need for water and a need for electric power.

The chief industry in the Imperial Valley is the raising of vegetables. The farmers' fields are now irrigated with water from the Colorado River. Farmers in Arizona, on the other side of the Colorado River, want a larger share of this water. In the future there won't be enough for both groups. But soon the California farmers may have access to the underground water. Then, the Arizona farmers can use all the water they want from the Colorado.

Desalting the underground water would not be difficult. Since the water reaches the earth's surface in the form of steam jets, simply cooling the steam would produce pure water. This water would be ready for drinking or for irrigating crops. The jets of steam could turn the turbines of electric power generators. The result would be a vast supply of low-cost electricity for homes and factories.

There would be no danger of running out of steam. Water from the ocean could be channeled to the area and allowed to trickle into the underground reservoir to replace water used. There is enough heat underground to turn water into steam for thousands of years.

1. In Southern California, one hot-water pocket lies under the fertile but dry
    a. Rhine Valley.   c. Imperial Valley.
    b. desert.   d. Colorado River.

2. The word in the last paragraph that means *to flow slowly* is

    _____ .

3. The words "on the other side of the Colorado River" in paragraph 3 describe

    _____ .

4. While it is not directly stated, the article suggests that
    a. some states need more water than they have.
    b. all states have more than enough water now.
    c. states should take water away from each other.

5. Underground water reaches the earth's surface in the form of
    a. electricity.
    b. steam jets.
    c. mineral water.

6. On the whole, this article tells about
    a. making use of underground reservoirs.
    b. the farmers who live in California.
    c. turbines of electric power generators.

7. Which statement does this article lead you to believe?
    a. Farmers from all over the States want to share the Colorado River.
    b. The farmers of Arizona are not interested in using more water now.
    c. The farmers of California and Arizona have argued about water rights.

8. Why would there be no danger of running out of steam?
    a. Water from the ocean could be used to drill new pockets.
    b. Water from the ocean could be channeled to the area.
    c. Water from the ocean now flows into the area.

9. Think about the concept for this group of articles. Which statement seems true both for the article and for the concept?
    a. It is not possible to take water from underground reservoirs in Italy.
    b. Huge underground reservoirs are located only in Southern California.
    c. Other areas may turn to their underground reservoirs for pure water.

Sharing the South Pole

The International Geophysical Year (IGY) lasted from July 1, 1957, to December 31, 1958. It was a time set aside by sixty-six nations for study of the earth and its environment. A major part of the IGY had to do with research projects in Antarctica. Few scientists had ever worked in Antarctica, so little was known about that continent.

During the IGY, scientists from twelve nations worked in Antarctica. Geologists recorded earthquakes, mapped mountains, and took samples of rocks. Meteorologists measured winds and temperatures. They learned much about how weather at the South Pole affects weather in other parts of the world.

For the benefit of science, the nations which had previously claimed parts of Antarctica set aside their claims. Boundary lines marked on the maps of Antarctica were ignored. Scientists were free to go where they pleased and to set up research stations wherever stations were needed. They were free to visit the stations set up by other nations and to exchange information.

This experiment in scientific cooperation between nations was so successful that it led to a new kind of treaty. The Antarctic Treaty, signed in Washington, D.C., in 1959 made Antarctica a free area. As long as their purposes are peaceful, people of all nations can now visit Antarctica. For thirty years, no nation will try to claim part of the icy continent as its own.

Today, Antarctica is the only free area on the earth. It is possible that the South Pole continent will always be a free area. It may be the first of many areas where people of different nations will work together for the good of all people.

1. A major part of the IGY had to do with research projects in
   a. Australia.
   c. Washington.
   b. Antarctica.
   d. the Arctic.

2. The words in paragraph 3 that mean *the borders of something* are

   _____ _____ .

3. The words "from twelve nations" in paragraph 2 refer to

   _____ .

4. While it is not directly stated, the article suggests that
   a. meteorologists were the only persons free to go where they pleased.
   b. scientists from Antarctica went to twelve nations.
   c. the nations were pleased with the results of their experiment.

5. No nation will try to claim part of the icy continent as its own for
   a. thirty years.
   b. twelve months.
   c. sixty years.

6. On the whole, the article tells about
   a. an experiment in scientific cooperation.
   b. earth and its environment marked on maps.
   c. meteorologists who measure temperatures.

7. Which statement does this article lead you to believe?
   a. Geologists and meteorologists are not really scientists anymore.
   b. Scientists think all scientific knowledge should be kept secret.
   c. Scientists are glad to share their knowledge with each other.

8. Why was so little known about the icy continent?
   a. No one knew where the boundaries were.
   b. Few scientists had ever worked there.
   c. Dangerous beasts kept people away from the shores.

9. Think about the concept for this group of articles. Which statement seems true both for the article and for the concept?
   a. Someday all peoples may cooperate in more and more fields.
   b. Someday all peoples of the world will become scientists.
   c. Someday all peoples may fight over the icy continents.

Games Mathematicians Play

There are many similarities between business competition and a card game such as bridge or poker. In each case both sides want to win. Neither side can learn all the secrets of the other side. Poker players can only guess what cards their opponents hold. A manufacturer can only guess what new products a competitor is bringing out.

The outcome of any competition depends partly on luck. It also depends on strategies the competitors use. Both the poker player and the manufacturer must make decisions based on their guesses about what their opponents will do next. Each must understand that the other might be bluffing.

It took a mathematician to translate this kind of competition into numbers and formulas and create a new branch of mathematics called Game Theory. The creator of Game Theory was John Von Neumann, who also helped to de- velop the atomic bomb.

Von Neumann's Game Theory makes a card game serve as a mathematical model of a real-life problem such as business competition. Mathematicians analyze the moves that a player can make. They also analyze the moves the opponent can make. They can then advise the businesses on their best strategy. They may even be able to predict the outcome of the "game."

Game Theory is used today to predict ups and downs in the nation's economy and to advise manufacturers when to bring out a new product. In years to come, Game Theory may be used to attack social problems that involve competition.

There is even a chance that Game Theory could eliminate war by providing a framework for discussion between nations in disagreement. Mathematicians who play games may prove to be the peacemakers of tomorrow's world.

FIND THE ANSWERS

1. The peacemakers of tomorrow's world may be
   a. opponents.
   b. mathematicians.
   c. business people.
   d. manufacturers.

2. The word in sentence 4 that means *one who is on the opposite side in a game* is

   _____ .

3. The words "a new branch of mathematics" in paragraph 3 refer to the

   _____ _____ .

4. While it is not directly stated, the article suggests that
   a. wars are one stage in the competition between nations.
   b. a game can cause wars between many nations.
   c. social problems are too difficult for mathematics.

5. John Von Neumann also helped to develop the
   a. game of bridge.
   b. way to bluff.
   c. atomic bomb.

6. On the whole, the article tells about
   a. the difference between a card game and business competition.
   b. a new branch of mathematics that can be used in many ways.
   c. manufacturers who must make decisions about their competitors.

7. Which statement does the article lead you to believe?
   a. The Game Theory could be used in many different areas.
   b. Only manufacturers are allowed to use the Game Theory.
   c. The Game Theory will be used like a weapon in an attack.

8. Why are there similarities between business competition and card games?
   a. Both sides want to win.
   b. Neither side can keep secrets.
   c. Both sides use mathematics.

9. Think about the concept for this group of articles. Which statement seems true both for the article and for the concept?
   a. A card game cannot serve as a model of real-life problems.
   b. Mathematicians are too limited to advise business on strategy.
   c. Planning and good sense may rule the world one day.

The Speed-Up
That Will Slow Time

Albert Einstein's famous Theory of Relativity states that time, like height, width, and breadth, is a dimension. These four dimensions are not fixed and unchangeable. They change as speed of movement changes. The only measurement in the universe that is fixed and unchangeable is the speed of light in a vacuum. That speed is 186,281 miles per second.

According to Einstein's theory, when the speed of a moving object increases, the object shrinks and becomes heavier. For the object, time passes more slowly. At speeds achieved in the past, these changes were too small to be noticeable.

At the greatest speeds achieved today, the changes are still very small. A jet plane traveling 1,400 miles per hour is only ten billionths of an inch shorter than the same plane on the ground. A clock aboard an artificial satellite traveling five miles per second loses only one hundredth of a second per year compared to a clock on the earth's surface.

It is only when a moving object approaches the speed of light that fantastic things happen. At 93,000 miles per second a 20-foot-long spacecraft would shrink to 17 feet. Aboard a spacecraft speeding toward the stars at 160,000 miles per second, time would pass just half as fast as time passes on earth. Two years on the spacecraft would be equal to four years on the earth's surface.

What an adventure awaits the astronauts of the future! They may travel so fast that shapes and measurements change. Even stranger, time will slow down.

Albert Einstein was a bold adventurer in the world of mathematics. From his views of the relationship between space and time came the knowledge that will help people explore distant planets and stars.

FIND THE ANSWERS

1. The speed of light in a vacuum is
   a. 222,246 miles per hour.
   b. 100,000 miles per hour.
   c. 281,186 miles per second.
   d. 186,281 miles per second.

2. The word in paragraph 1 that means *a measurement of time, breadth, width, or height* is _____.

3. The words "a bold adventurer in the world of mathematics" in paragraph 6 describe _____ _____.

4. While it is not directly stated, the article suggests that
   a. the speed of light has no effect on measurements.
   b. the only way we travel is at the speed of light.
   c. we cannot yet travel at the speed of light.

5. When the speed of a moving object increases, the object
   a. stretches and becomes stronger.
   b. shrinks and becomes heavier.
   c. swells and becomes lighter.

6. On the whole, the article tells about
   a. the relationship between speed and time.
   b. shapes and measurements that keep changing.
   c. clocks aboard an artificial satellite.

7. Which statement does this article lead you to believe?
   a. Time passes twice as fast on earth as it does in space.
   b. Time passes the same way for all, in space or on earth.
   c. Future astronauts will not age as quickly as people on earth.

8. Why were Einstein's views of space and time important?
   a. They helped people learn about the speed of light.
   b. They gave people the chance to build moving objects.
   c. They gave people the knowledge to make space travel possible.

9. Think about the concept for this group of articles. Which statement seems true both for the article and for the concept?
   a. People are beginning to plan further travel into space.
   b. Most people agree that our spacecraft will be too short for high speeds.
   c. Albert Einstein was the world's finest spacecraft designer.

Say Goodby to Traffic Jams

Today, transportation is one of the major problems of large cities. Rush hours often create huge traffic jams. Exhaust fumes from thousands of automobiles pollute the air. In hopes of solving these problems, some scientists and engineers are considering new ways of transportation for the city of the future.

In tomorrow's city, people may travel short distances of a mile or less on a transporter belt or "moving walk." Passengers will be able to walk on and off at any point just as safely as people today step on and off an escalator.

Tomorrow's automobile may be changed greatly from today's models. It might be small and square and run on electric batteries, which will produce little noise and no fumes. However, most people will no longer own their own cars. Instead, they will ride in self-service taxicabs stationed underground at different points along a city's main thoroughfares. To unlock the door of one, people will put a credit card into a slot. To go to the suburbs, they will drive the cab themselves. To travel about in the city, they will simply tell a computer station where they want to go. Then, an automatic driving system will move them to their destination.

In the city of the future, many people may travel on a very fast underground train. Perhaps they will ride in electronically controlled "pods" that run on monorails. These "pods" could carry people from their homes to any destination they wish.

For people in the cities of tomorrow, traffic jams and exhaust fumes will be a thing of the past.

1. Tomorrow's automobile may be
   - a. large and round.
   - b. small and square.
   - c. little and pointed.
   - d. wide and triangular.

2. The word in paragraph 1 that means *make dirty or unclean* is

   _____.

3. The words "stationed underground at different points along a city's main

   thoroughfares" in paragraph 3 refer to _____.

4. While it is not directly stated, the article suggests that
   - a. transporter belts will be very dangerous to use.
   - b. people will no longer be able to go where they wish.
   - c. traveling in the future may be more pleasant.

5. People of the future may travel
   - a. by more automatic means.
   - b. in self-service "pads."
   - c. only by underground trains.

6. On the whole, the article tells about
   - a. exhaust fumes in huge traffic jams.
   - b. transportation in the city of the future.
   - c. people who must travel underground.

7. Which statement does this article lead you to believe?
   - a. Computers of the future will do less work than those of today.
   - b. Computers can be used only for figuring out traffic patterns.
   - c. Driving could be safer when it is controlled by computers.

8. Why would a person put his credit card into a slot?
   - a. In order to drive the electronic "pad."
   - b. In order to unlock the door of the self-service taxicab.
   - c. In order to store the credit card until it is needed.

9. Think about the concept for this group of articles. Which statement seems true both for the article and for the concept?
   - a. Huge traffic jams and exhaust fumes will always be a problem in our cities.
   - b. Cities of the future could be cleaner than they are today.
   - c. The best idea might be to eliminate cities entirely.

Trash to Treasure

Almost every filled-up trash can contains small amounts of gold, silver, iron, copper, lead, tin, zinc, and aluminum, as well as rubber, plastics, cloth, and paper. These materials can be salvaged and made into new products.

In the past, Americans have thrown away vast amounts of valuable substances. It was cheaper for manufacturers to buy new raw materials than to reclaim used ones. But today it costs money to dispose of refuse. Cities must deal with mountains of trash every day. Attempts to burn this refuse add to air pollution. The trash can be buried, but many cities are running out of land to use for burying refuse.

Salvaging used matter would solve not one problem but three. It would provide new supplies of substances like metals. It would help preserve the world's natural resources. It would dispose of all but a small amount of the trash that must now be burned or buried.

In the long run, reclaiming used materials may be the only way to keep the earth from turning into one vast trash heap.

Scientists and engineers are now developing new methods for reclaiming metals from refuse. Eventually they expect to salvage 7 million dollars worth of gold and silver every year. Even more valuable will be the vast amount of steel reclaimed from tin cans. Old bottles will be ground up, melted, and used to make new glass products. Garbage will be turned into fertilizer to enrich soil used for growing new food crops. One inventor has even developed a method for compressing garbage into solid building blocks.

In the future, people may learn to reuse, over and over, the stuff that they now use once and then throw away. The treasures from the trash piles should pay the costs of new methods of salvage and disposal.

1. One inventor developed a method for compressing garbage into
    a. a vast trash heap.   c. new glass products.
    b. fertilizer.   d. solid building blocks.

2. The word in paragraph 1 that means *saved or reclaimed* is

    _____ .

3. The words "reclaimed from tin cans" in paragraph 4 describe the vast amount

    of _____ .

4. While it is not directly stated, the article suggests that
    a. every garbage pail in America is filled with gold.
    b. disposing of garbage is becoming a serious problem.
    c. the world's natural resources will never be a problem.

5. Some garbage can be turned into
    a. fertilizer.
    b. reclaimed metals.
    c. food crops.

6. On the whole, the article tells about
    a. reclaiming valuable materials from the trash piles.
    b. salvaging trash from valuable materials thrown away.
    c. scientists and engineers who look for gold and silver.

7. Which statement does this article lead you to believe?
    a. It is easy to tell when products are made from salvaged material.
    b. In the future, there will be money to be made from reclaiming trash.
    c. Reclaiming trash is already a major industry.

8. Why did manufacturers prefer to buy new materials?
    a. It was cheaper.
    b. There was not enough trash.
    c. Trash was too hard to find.

9. Think about the concept for this group of articles. Which statement seems true
    both for the article and for the concept?
    a. The only thing to do with trash is to bury it.
    b. There will never be any profit from salvaging trash or garbage.
    c. Builders may use compressed garbage to build houses someday.

Art — But What Kind?

There may be an art explosion ahead.

People will be working shorter hours, taking longer vacations, and retiring at an earlier age. They will have more time, and probably more money, for activities not directly connected with making a living. Under these circumstances, many people will take a great interest in art.

What kind of art might the future bring? The questions can't be answered with certainty. Art is always a product of its own time and it changes as life changes.

It is possible, however, that the future will bring a new appreciation for the art of the past. In an age of mass production and synthetic materials, people may place a higher value on handicrafts, things created by hand from natural materials. People may want to see pictures that suggest an "old-fashioned"

kind of beauty which has become rare in the world they know.

It is also possible that in the future much of the art we know today will disappear. New art forms may be so exciting and full of motion that no one will want to look at a flat picture or a sculpture that stands still.

It is certain that tomorrow's artists will use new substances in new ways. The unusual materials are likely to be combined with elements that were once thought of as separate. Light patterns will combine with sound. Color and form will combine with motion. These elements will reach out and surround the viewers. They won't just *look* at art; they will experience it.

What new kind of beauty will tomorrow's artists create? The people who know most about art forms and the history of art will only predict that there will be new and surprising things.

1. In the future, artists may combine color and form with
   - a. natural materials.
   - b. synthetics.
   - c. the viewer.
   - d. motion.

2. The word in the last paragraph that means *tell in advance* is

   _____ .

3. The words "a product of its own time" in paragraph 3 describe

   _____ .

4. While it is not directly stated, the article suggests that
   - a. all artists paint the same way today.
   - b. art of the past is still admired.
   - c. no one likes "old-fashioned" art.

5. People may place a higher value on
   - a. handicrafts.
   - b. synthetic materials.
   - c. flat pictures.

6. On the whole, the article tells about
   - a. the changing world of art.
   - b. sculptures that move.
   - c. new materials in history.

7. Which statement does this article lead you to believe?
   - a. Handicrafts will be the only true art of the future.
   - b. It is easy to predict the art forms and materials of the future.
   - c. Artists will need to know more than how to paint and carve.

8. Why will viewers "experience" art someday?
   - a. Everyone will be given materials to create their own art.
   - b. The elements of color, form, and motion will surround him.
   - c. Art will be required in all public schools.

9. Think about the concept for this group of articles. Which statement seems true both for the article and for the concept?
   - a. Not everyone will be pleased with the world of the future.
   - b. Tomorrow's artists will only create art in a computer.
   - c. It is always easy to understand new art forms.

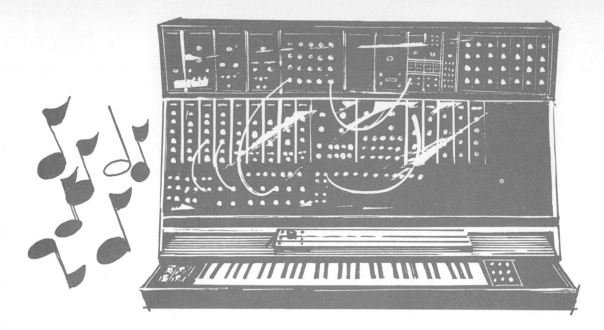

"Switched On"

An electronic synthesizer has keys like piano keys. Otherwise, no one might guess by looking at it that it had anything to do with music. It resembles something between a computer and a telephone switchboard. It is a thing of switches, flashing lights, and dangling wires.

This strange instrument looks as if it might turn out punched cards or paper tape printed with mathematical symbols. Instead, it makes music. It can produce sounds like those of a flute, a violin, or a human voice. It can also produce new sounds that are not at all like human voices or ordinary musical instruments.

Within the electronic synthesizer are devices that produce a changing electronic current. This current is translated into sounds which are changed in different ways by filters and volume controls. The sound is recorded on tape after which it may be played again so that more sounds may be added. Other effects may be produced by playing the tape faster to raise the pitch of the sound, or slower to lower the pitch.

Today, some composers are turning to new instruments such as the electronic synthesizer. They are writing music that human musicians cannot play. The electronic synthesizer gives composers command of the entire range of tones which the human ear can hear.

Before long, music-lovers may be going to a new kind of concert. Instead of enjoying a famous soloist or a hundred musicians playing ordinary instruments under the direction of a renowned conductor, tomorrow's concert audience may face an empty stage. Tape recorders will feed electronically produced music into loudspeakers hung around the auditorium. The music will surround each listener. There may be nothing much to see, but that should make it easier for the listener to concentrate on the strange but beautiful new sounds he or she will hear.

FIND THE ANSWERS

1. An electronic synthesizer has
   a. synthetic wires.
   b. mathematical symbols.
   c. a limited range.
   d. keys like a piano.

2. The word in the last paragraph that means *gather one's attention* is

   _____ .

3. The words "like those of a flute, a violin, or a human voice" in paragraph 2

   describe the sounds of an _____

   _____ .

4. While it is not directly stated, the article suggests that
   a. some composers find the electronic synthesizer a challenge.
   b. most composers will not use an instrument like the synthesizer.
   c. synthesizers cannot produce as great a range of tones as the violin.

5. Tomorrow's concert audience may face
   a. a stage full of musicians.
   b. an empty stage.
   c. a computer.

6. On the whole, the article tells about
   a. music produced by an electronic instrument.
   b. loudspeakers hanging around auditoriums.
   c. musicians who play several instruments.

7. Which statement does this article lead you to believe?
   a. People are willing to listen to new sounds.
   b. Most composers prefer more musicians on stage.
   c. A famous conductor is more popular than a famous soloist.

8. Why is the sound recorded on tape?
   a. It can help the composers remember what they wrote.
   b. It can be played again and more sounds added.
   c. It can be used to direct a hundred musicians.

9. Think about the concept for this group of articles. Which statement seems true
   both for the article and for the concept?
   a. Music of tomorrow may no longer be music as we know it now.
   b. All music from now on will be composed on switchboards.
   c. Flashing lights and dangling wires are piano keys.

Fill in your record chart after each test. Beside the page numbers, put a one for each correct question. Put zero in the box of each question you missed. At the far right, put your total. Nine is a perfect score for each test.

When you finish all the tests in a concept, total your scores by question. The highest possible score for each question in one concept is the number of stories.

When you have taken several tests, check to see which question you get right each time. Which ones are you missing? Find the places where you need help. For example, if you are missing Question 3 often, ask for help in learning to use directing words.

As you begin each concept, copy the chart onto lined paper. Down the left side are the test page numbers. Across the top are the question numbers and the kinds of questions. For example, each Question 1 in this book asks you to recall a fact. Your scores for each question show how well you are learning each skill.

Your Reading Scores

Concept I

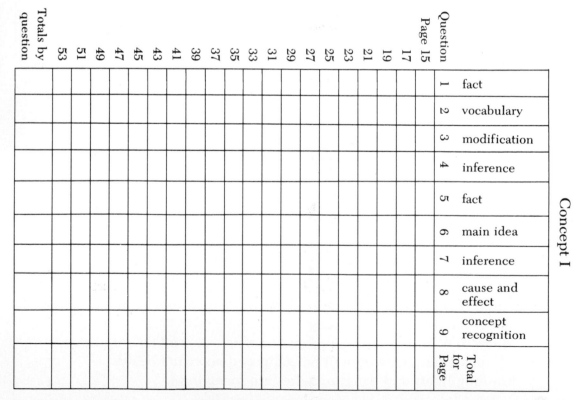

Question Page	1 fact	2 vocabulary	3 modification	4 inference	5 fact	6 main idea	7 inference	8 cause and effect	9 concept recognition	Total for Page
15										
17										
19										
21										
23										
25										
27										
29										
31										
33										
35										
37										
39										
41										
43										
45										
47										
49										
51										
53										
Totals by question										

Your Reading Scores

Concept III

Question	fact 1	vocabulary 2	modification 3	inference 4	fact 5	main idea 6	inference 7	cause and effect 8	concept recognition 9	Total for Page
Page 103										
105										
107										
109										
111										
113										
115										
117										
119										
121										
123										
125										
127										
129										
131										
133										
135										
137										
139										
141										
Totals by question										

Your Reading Scores

Concept II

Question	fact 1	vocabulary 2	modification 3	inference 4	fact 5	main idea 6	inference 7	cause and effect 8	concept recognition 9	Total for Page
Page 59										
61										
63										
65										
67										
69										
71										
73										
75										
77										
79										
81										
83										
85										
87										
89										
91										
93										
95										
97										
Totals by question										

Your Reading Scores — Concept IV

Question	Page 147	149	151	153	155	157	159	161	163	165	167	169	171	173	175	177	179	181	183	185	Totals by question
1 fact																					
2 vocabulary																					
3 modification																					
4 inference																					
5 fact																					
6 main idea																					
7 inference																					
8 cause and effect																					
9 concept recognition																					
Total for Page																					

WORDS YOU WILL NEED

These are words and names that are hard to read. Learn how to say each word. Find the word in the story. Learn the meaning. Use the word in a sentence of your own. The words are only listed once. You will need the words you learned to read the stories that follow.

p. 14
actually
astronauts
beliefs
bulged
colleagues
computers
curve
definitely
discussed
distance
gather
gravitational
hemisphere
information
mathematician

measurement
orbit
perigee
realize
regular
research
satellite
soaring
spacecrafts
Ann Eckels Bailie
Silly Putty
Vanguard I

p. 16
advantage
antislavery

classified
community
editor
influenced
journals
practical
publication
publish
real estate
results
Juvenile Miscellany
The Los Angeles Sentinel

p. 18
accurate

astronomer
contradicted
eventually
mathematician
orbited
position
ridiculed
satellites
scanning
solar
system
theory
vast
Copernicus
Galileo
Ptolemy

p. 20
astronauts
distortion
effective
exploration
flickering
functions
gravitational
hinder
lens
markers
patterns
project
turbulence
Gordon Cooper
Himalayas

Mercury-Atlas
Project Mercury

p. 22
bounties
domestic
erosion
European
flourished
immunity
invaders
myxomatosis
nourished
once-productive
pelts
topsoil

188

twelfth
Australia

p. 24
additional
boll
borers
destructive
experiments
gypsy
hazards
insecticides
Japanese
severely
source
sugarcane
troublesome
weevil
Louisiana
Mississippi Valley

p. 26
affairs
agencies
allotment
clung
division
individual
motels
policy
poverty
reservations
reversed
tribal
tribe
*General Allotment
   Act*
*Indian Reorgani-
   zation Act*

p. 28
abolishing
barriers
castes
democracy
distinction
effectively
estates
idle
independent
untouchability
untouchables

Brahmins
Hindus
India

p. 30
communism
established
influences
nobles
restless
serfs
toppled
Baltic Sea
Czar Nicholas II
*Czar Peter the
   Great*
Leningrad
Russia
Sweden

p. 32
controlled
domination
empire
granted
leadership
monarch
occupied
reclaim
reluctant
retained
throughout
Africa
Asia
*British
   Common-
   wealth*

p. 34
average
drought
farmland
obscured
ochre-colored
prospered
rainfall
resembled
transformed
varied
Dakotas
Illinois
Kansas

Nebraska
New York

p. 36
continent
establish
expanded
expanses
identical
international
timetables
Canada

p. 38
area
depression
destruction
elevated
naturalist
quake
resist
series
severe
temporarily
Boston
*John James
   Audubon*
Kentucky
Lake Eulalie
*New Madrid,
   Missouri*
New Orleans
Tennessee

p. 40
eruptions
fragments
mapmakers
masses
process
site
submerged
vent
Aleutians
Guam
Hawaii
Myojin
Pacific Ocean
Tokyo

p. 42
automatically

circuit
computers
contraption
current
electronic
forecasters
loom
marvels
preview
textile
translated
Jacquard

p. 44
calculate
complex
dealt
energy
extremely
foresee
formula
indirect
mass
physics
published
spare
Swiss
theories
uranium
Albert Einstein
Atlantic

p. 46
aircraft
airliners
capacity
congestion
inconvenience
jet-powered
prewar
relocate
require
soared
taxiways
upsurge
*Washington,
   D.C.*

p. 48
antennae
areas
artificial

audience
biology
bionic
dolphin
fascinated
handicapped
instance
knowledge
mechanical
muscles
original
porpoise
propellers
series
sonar

p. 50
earliest
fragment
hobbyists
ornamental
primitive
tiles
Babylonia
Egypt

p. 52
calculators
conventional
converts
delicate
electron
original
oscilloscope
radar
range
reproduction
transforms
version

pp. 54-56
agreeably
amplifier
annual
appreciation
calmly
ceremony
countdown
devices
frantically
frequent
gingerly

greasy
grubby
ignored
immediately
issues
nuisance
operate
perch
perpetual
petunia
probably
referred
rejected
runny
samples
slightly
stereo
strolled
tinkered
unbolted
unmanned
urge
weird-looking
whirring
Eleanor
Erector
Golden Gloves
Harry Heimer
Horace Beeson
Little League
Popular Mechanics
Thermothrockle
U.S. Patent Office

p. 58
advantage
constant
exile
friction
homeland
preserved
province
religion
resented
resettle
resistance
supervision
Arabs
*European
   Crusaders*
Hebrews
Israel

crescent
enforce
intricate
profitable
repeatedly
reservation
reshaping
silversmithing
silverwork
territory
warfare
wavy
Arizona
Colonel
Kit Carson
Fort Sumner
Navaho Indians
New Mexico

pp. 98-100
accomplished
alas
blanched
courtyard
desolate
enchantment
exhausted
expressed
haughtily
impart
intent
lamenting
moreover
outwit
quest
repulsive
restore
reunited
sidling
sire
sixteenth
slew
stairway
stepdaughters
summon
tempted
thereupon
turret
urns
whisk
woe
wrath

p. 102
breakthrough
census
consult
deteriorates
documents
historical
image
manuscripts
microfilmed
reduces
storage
user
King Henry VII
Rome
United States
  Census
Vatican Library

p. 104
arthritis
capitol
multimillion
publishers
successful
Afro-American
Benjamin
  Banneker
Booker T
  Washington
Dr. Charles Drew
Dr. Daniel Hale
  Williams
Dr. Percy Julian
George
  Washington
  Carver
Granville T.
  Woods
Jan Matzeliger

p. 106
charred
exercise
flammable
nonflammable
overconfident
per
redesigning
simulated
timetable
Apollo

Cape Kennedy
Edward White
Gemini
Roger Chaffee
Virgil Grissom

p. 108
concerning
cooperatively
duplication
meteorological
progressed
representatives
wasteful
Chairman Nikita
  Khrushchev
Friendship 7
John Glenn
Moscow
President John F.
  Kennedy
Soviet Union
Space Age
Vostok I
Yuri Gagarin

p. 110
alewife
coho
conservation
conservationists
decreased
fisherman
foresight
hydroelectric
overfishing
perils
pollution
spawn
thrived
turbines
upriver
Great Lakes
Lake Michigan

p. 112
devices
environment
exhausts
extinction
fumes
poisonous

requiring
respiratory
sewage
Industrial Age

p. 114
anthropologist
authority
conflict
consulted
emerging
foreign-aid
minimum
progress
relic
sacred
societies
unindustrialized
Ashanti
Peace Corps

p. 116
accommodate
bloody
corresponded
dialects
link
national
Hindi

p. 118
densely
emphasizing
erode
financial
investors
lure
technical
unemployment
Caribbean
Operation
  Bootstrap
Puerto Rican

p. 120
apply
competition
competitor
consumer
nonmember
recent
tripled

Belgium
European
  Common
  Market
France
Luxembourg
Netherlands

p. 122
accurately
aerial
altitudes
constantly
continental
focused
satellite
scanner
telescope
Landsat

p. 124
association
pulpwood
synthetics
woodlots

p. 126
agency
eroded
formed
long-range
purposes
restored
sources
tributaries
widespread
Alabama
Tennessee River
  Basin

p. 128
disastrous
excess
floodwaters
levee
mesh
permanently
preserving
reinforced
suction
Baton Rouge,
  Louisiana

Cairo, Illinois

p. 130
alloy
circumference
computing
elements
gyroscope
krypton
meter
one-millionth
platinum-iridium
precision
unit
Barcelona, Spain
Dunkirk, Belgium
General
  Conference
  of Weights and
  Measures
Paris

p. 132
actuaries
estimated
insured
life-span
occupations
predicts
probability
statistics
Theory of
  Probability

p. 134
air-cushion
all-purpose
downward
Finnish
high-pressure
operating
resemble
uneconomical
Christopher
  Cockerell
English Channel
Hovercraft
Norway
San Francisco Bay
Scotland
Toivo Kaario